WORLD BANK STAFF OCCASIONAL PAPERS ☐ NUMBER TWENTY-ONE

Manuel Zymelman

The Economic Evaluation of Vocational Training Programs

with the assistance of
Alan Woodruff, Morris Horowitz, and Irwin Herrnstadt

Published for the World Bank
THE JOHNS HOPKINS UNIVERSITY PRESS
BALTIMORE AND LONDON

102525

Library of Congress Cataloging in Publication Data:

Zymelman, Manuel.
    Economic evaluation of vocational training programs.
    (World Bank staff occasional papers; no. 21)
    Bibliography: p. 117
    1. Vocational education 2. Education—Economic aspects. I. International Bank
for Reconstruction and Development. II. Title. III. Series.
LC1044.Z95   374′.013   76-4868
ISBN 0-8018-1855-9

Foreword

I would like to explain why the World Bank does research work and why this research is published. We feel an obligation to look beyond the projects that we help finance toward the whole resource allocation of an economy and the effectiveness of the use of those resources. Our major concern, in dealings with member countries, is that all scarce resources—including capital, skilled labor, enterprise, and know-how—should be used to their best advantage. We want to see policies that encourage appropriate increases in the supply of savings, whether domestic or international. Finally, we are required by our Articles, as well as by inclination, to use objective economic criteria in all our judgments.

These are our preoccupations, and these, one way or another, are the subjects of most of our research work. Clearly, they are also the proper concern of anyone who is interested in promoting development, and so we seek to make our research papers widely available. In doing so, we have to take the risk of being misunderstood. Although these studies are published by the Bank, the views expressed and the methods explored should not necessarily be considered to represent the Bank's views or policies. Rather, they are offered as a modest contribution to the great discussion on how to advance the economic development of the underdeveloped world.

ROBERT S. MCNAMARA
President
The World Bank

Preface

In recognition of the fact that a trained labor force is one of the essentials for economic development, a major objective of the World Bank is to assist developing countries in meeting their need for industrial skills. Vocational training is an obvious solution to the shortage of skilled workers, but the choice of specific program is less clear. Industrial crafts can be taught in different ways: through vocational schools, apprenticeships, skill centers, and various combinations of on- and off-the-job training. Which of these methods should be adopted in developing countries? Is there one which is more cost effective than the others?

The present study by Manuel Zymelman attempts to answer these questions. He reviews the evidence already available in the literature and deals with evaluations of different types of training in developed and developing countries. Different methods of on-the-job, off-the-job, and combined types of training are thoroughly discussed, as well as the advantages and disadvantages of each. He then presents a detailed theoretical discussion of economic and institutional factors that affect the selection of a mode of training. The final chapter provides a methodology for analyzing and evaluating proposals for establishing a vocational training program.

This study represents an important step in our research effort to increase the efficiency of educational and training systems in developing countries. Recent debates have challenged the traditional reliance on vocational schools and tended to create a bias in favor of on-the-job programs. The author finds no evidence to support the claim for a clear-cut superiority of one method over another. Instead, by presenting a general framework for analyzing modes of training, he provides academicians and practitioners with a tool that will enable them to evaluate each case on its own merit.

The author wishes to thank Necat Erder, Mats Hultin, and Jean-Pierre Jallade of the World Bank staff for their valuable comments.

The views and interpretations in this book are those of the author and should not be attributed to the World Bank, to its affiliated organizations, or to any individual acting in their behalf.

DUNCAN S. BALLANTINE
Director, Education Department

Washington, D.C.
April 1976

Contents

Figures

Tables

The Economic Evaluation
of Vocational
Training Programs

I

Introduction

Training for industrial occupations in vocational schools is a comparatively recent phenomenon. Until the 19th century apprenticeship and informal training developed the skills for most manual occupations, largely through imitation and association with a master, often for many years. For a time the Industrial Revolution tended to lower the level of skill required by the working force, but gradually the methods of mass production brought a diversification of functions and greater specialization. With technological advances, analytical and communication skills were required as well as more theoretical knowledge. Informal training alone was no longer enough. A formal classroom setting was needed in which to teach the new skills and provide an alternative form of general education to those who did not follow the academic route to white-collar or managerial jobs.

Pressured by the industrial sector's growing demand for skilled workers, governments began to provide not only specific vocational training but also general education—reading, writing, arithmetic, and science. In spite of the rapid development of vocational schools, however, the majority of workers continued to acquire their skills through informal apprenticeship or in-plant programs. The relative merits of these methods of vocational training have only recently been questioned.

Since World War II automation and unemployment in developed countries and the demand for skilled manpower to develop newly founded nations have made it necessary to determine the most effective methods of training. In developed economies rapid technological change required workers with more flexibility and a deeper theoretical knowledge of their occupation. The abolition of some occupations and the creation of new

3

employment opportunities necessitated training or retraining workers in a relatively short time. New systems of training in schools, factories, and skill centers were developed to accommodate to the changing labor market. Developing nations, confronted with a scarcity of skilled manpower, have looked for ways to expand the supply quickly by training workers at rates unknown before. They have for the most part copied or adapted the three basic methods used in developed countries: training on the job, both formal and informal; training off the job in schools, training centers, or places of work; and combined types of training such as apprenticeship with formal instruction off the job, on-the-job training with some related instruction, and cooperative-work training.

Comparison of Training Methods

Each method offers certain advantages and disadvantages. With on-the-job training the trainee is assured a job and income and does not have to be concerned about finding work after finishing the course. This type of training is feasible only when there are job openings and the ratio of trainees to employees is small. Another limitation is that the training might focus on a narrowly defined skill that cannot be used in other occupations.

Classroom training, whether in schools, factories, or skill centers, has the advantages of accommodating a large number of students and offering a variety of courses, full or part time, throughout the day and week. The drawbacks are that it requires a minimum number of students and trained instructors. Such programs tend to become inflexible, especially when expensive equipment is needed, and there is no guarantee of employment after the course is completed.

Apprenticeship is sometimes the only way to acquire the needed credentials for a job, but the training period may be unduly long. Cooperative work-study programs provide income and experience while allowing the trainee to finish high school, but they require close coordination of the roles of school and employer. The benefits of other combined methods of training are similarly balanced by certain drawbacks.

Of all the methods available the favorite choice of developing countries is the vocational school. It offers the most accessible type of training and is the least encumbered by administrative and operational obstacles.

Before more resources are poured into vocational schools, however, some basic questions need to be answered: Is this the most effective type of training? How do costs compare with those of other methods? Can other programs be readily substituted for vocational schools?

In an attempt to provide some answers a thorough search was made of the literature, and most available studies of industrial training were evaluated, fifty-four in all.[1] Surprisingly few deal directly with the above questions or attempt to compare methods; most concern developed countries only. A number of studies evaluate specific programs but do not delve thoroughly into costs and benefits. They fail to consider whether the measured benefits of a program derive from the quality of instruction or rather from the employment opportunities available. Nor is the efficiency of operation taken into account in discussing the cost of a given method. Other studies isolate and evaluate variables that influence the effectiveness of training. Seldom is this followed up by an analysis of the cost of offsetting the effect of these variables, such as setting up remedial programs to repair deficiencies in student backgrounds.

In industrial countries it is generally believed that costs of formal vocational training are higher than those of on-the-job training—although a detailed study in West Germany shows the opposite to be true. At the same time the training given by vocational schools is believed to be more effective than that received on the job.

Most studies done in developing nations compare the cost effectiveness of vocational and academic secondary schools and generally conclude that vocational schools are not profitable. This could be the result of inefficient operations, but it is believed to be primarily because there is little demand in the labor market for the training which was received. If, as some studies find, many vocational school graduates do not find jobs, is that because of faulty instruction or because they were trained for the wrong occupations? In the latter case a different mode of training would not alter the result unless the decisionmaking process that determines the content of instruction is corrected to conform with market conditions. In any event correcting the decisionmaking process may be cheaper than changing modes of training.

In other studies formal vocational schools show a high cost per graduate. This could result from a poor use of capacity and does not validate a claim that training outside of school is more profitable (assuming equal benefits). With a more efficient use of faculty and equipment the cost per student could change radically.

The survey of the literature thus raised more questions than it answered and uncovered no universally applicable solution to the problem of whether vocational school or on-the-job training is more effective. The fifty-four studies reviewed in Appendix C deal with specific situations, and their conclusions cannot be applied to training under markedly different conditions. Nor were the costs and benefits observed necessarily those of efficient operations. It is therefore impossible to determine the cost effectiveness of

1. See Appendix C.

any method on the basis of these studies, and there is no conclusive evidence that one type of training is superior to others.

Factors Affecting the Choice of Program

The issue then is not which method is more cost effective but rather under what circumstances one type should be chosen over another. The solution will vary with each situation and must be reached by a systematic exploration of the conditions under which one mode of training is more advantageous than another. Both economic and institutional factors will determine the choice. The decision to train workers off the job, on the job, or with some combination of the two methods will therefore depend on an analysis of all these factors.

The economic assessment of a training program will focus on the average cost per graduate, which is affected by the scale of operation, the existence of other programs on the same premises, and the nature of laboratories or workshops. When the technology requires high fixed costs, average costs will be high for a small number of people but will decrease if more students can be included in the program. Sometimes it is possible to lower the average cost of training by increasing the enrollment in related programs which share the same resources, thus increasing the utilization of facilities and equipment. The average cost of a program will therefore depend not only on enrollment but on the mix of programs offered by the institution. Optimal use of the facilities will also depend on the kind of equipment needed and the nature of instruction. The capacity of some laboratories can be expanded by the addition of a single machine to serve several students; in other cases a group of machines would be needed as a unit.

A firm's decision to offer training in the plant will depend to a large extent on the cost of training, the trainees' wages, and profitability to the firm. High wages make on-the-job training expensive and are more conducive to classroom training. Small differences between the wages of skilled and unskilled workers also militate against in-plant training. Loyalty to the firm may induce workers to accept lower wages, however, thus making in-plant training more profitable. Imperfections of the labor market such as lack of competition or restricted dissemination of market information tend to make in-plant training feasible. Companies will sometimes initiate training programs to generate goodwill or for political purposes. But the willingness to offer training can also be encouraged by government action in the form of subsidies and tax incentives, as well as the administrative machinery for allocating public resources.

Among the institutional factors that influence the choice of mode of training are such characteristics of the labor market as the rate of unemployment, level of wages, and the entry requirements for jobs. Regardless of the actual skill or knowledge necessary for the successful performance of a job, some occupations have standard prerequisites for entry. If a vocational school or apprenticeship certificate is widely deemed essential these types of training will be favored over other available means.

The attitude of firms and unions will sometimes limit the choice of method. If, rightly or wrongly, an industry is biased against vocational schools because of previous experience, there is little merit in expanding school capacity. A strong union may similarly take a stand that makes it difficult to attempt on-the-job training.

Another institutional factor critical to the success of any formal training program is the quality of instruction. The choice of program may then be determined by the availability of a well-planned curriculum, competent administrators, and teachers with both practical experience and pedagogical ability.

Methodology for Assessing Training Programs

A firm grasp of all the economic and institutional factors affecting existing or potential programs makes it possible to determine the most advantageous method of training in a given situation. Without empirical evidence to indicate the universal superiority of any one mode, the case for each country or region must be evaluated individually. To facilitate this evaluation process a gestalt approach is suggested that encompasses all the economic and institutional variables. The purpose of this book is to provide a methodology, based on theoretical analyses and practical experience, for the careful assessment of vocational training programs. The guidelines set forth should enable policymakers to evaluate proposals for vocational schools or other forms of training and choose the most effective program for a particular situation.

Chapter 2 presents a general discussion of on-the-job, off-the-job, and combined types of training and lists the advantages and disadvantages of each. This section offers a useful introduction for economists, educational administrators, and decisionmakers who are not experts in vocational training and therefore not well acquainted with the particular characteristics of these types of training.

Chapter 3 provides a theoretical analysis of all the factors that influence the choice of a mode of training. It includes a discussion of the economic factors affecting the cost of training: size of programs, the coexistence of related programs, the nature of the laboratories, and the urgency with which training is needed. The economic feasibility of in-plant training is considered, together with government economic policies to foster training by private enterprises. The concluding section deals with the effects of institutional factors. This chapter, like the preceding one, addresses those who are not experts on vocational education, and it supplies background information necessary to make a judicious selection of a method of training.

To evaluate the cost effectiveness of a mode of training for a given occupation, data are needed on program duration, specificity of courses and distribution of instructional time, cost of equipment, and the possibility of training within the place of work. Chapter 4 furnishes data on programs that are commonly found in vocational schools although they could also be conducted in other environments. The first set of tables shows the distribution of hours spent in the classroom on general academic work and related theory and in various laboratories, both shared and specific. Other data indicate the transferability of theoretical and practical instruction, that is, the extent to which it is applicable to different jobs in the same field. The second set of tables provides data on the approximate cost of laboratory equipment in 1972. Although these figures will rapidly become out of date, they indicate the relative cost of different laboratories and provide a basis for calculating the average cost of training. The final table shows the proportion of workers from selected occupations in the labor force of major industries.

A methodology for analyzing and evaluating a proposal for vocational training is presented in Chapter 5. A flow chart graphically displays the sequence of operations that will lead to a logical economic choice. Steps that are not self-explanatory are discussed in the text together with practical suggestions for achieving the best results.

2

Characteristics of Industrial Vocational Training

Just as there are many alternative methods of production, so too there are a variety of ways to teach manual skills, and one technique can often be substituted for another. For example, formal courses, including shop classes in vocational and technical schools, can be replaced by observation and practical experience. The effectiveness of any one method has to be decided on its own merits after consideration of the cost of training and the degree of skill desired. The net advantage of each alternative must be separately determined.

Two fundamentally different methods are used to train manual workers in industry. In one training is received while working in the production process; the other takes place in some other environment, off the job itself. In the former the individual is working on a specific job and simultaneously learning by doing. In the latter he may or may not be employed, but in either case he is trained outside the production process. Each of these two basic methods contains an array of discrete subgroups which may be summarized as follows:

A. Training on the job
1. Formal on-the-job training
2. Informal training
B. Training off the job
1. Location and/or sponsor
a. Public school
b. Work place or employer
c. Training center

Figure 1. Indifference Curves for Combinations of On- and Off-the-job Training

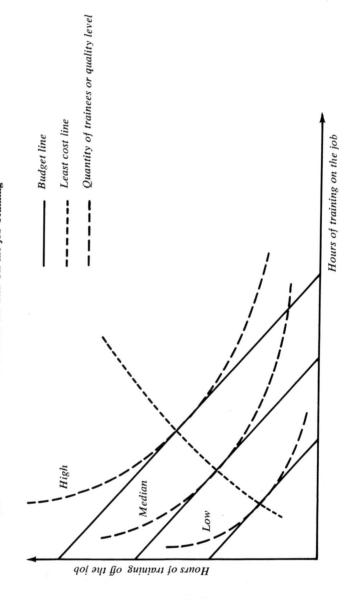

    d. Private proprietary school
    e. Equipment manufacturers
  2. Kind of classroom and/or course
    a. Shop class
    b. Classroom
      (i) Vocational (related instruction)
      (ii) Academic or nonvocational
C. Combined types of training
  1. Formal apprenticeship
  2. On-the-job training plus related instruction

Training on the job takes a variety of forms ranging from a highly organized program, with a definite curriculum and special instructors, to a loosely structured, informal helper-craftsman relationship. Nevertheless all these varieties involve trainees who are employed by the firm in which they are being trained. There need not be an explicit acknowledgment of a training relationship; the length of training and its content can vary with the needs of the employer and the learning speed or ability of the trainee. Training on the job is imparted by either another worker, a special instructor, or a supervisor who acts as an instructor by assigning tasks to the trainee and evaluating his performance.

Similarly there are many forms of training off the job that differ as to their timing, location, sponsorship, and course content. The training class can be held during or outside of the scheduled work day, part time or full time, in a shop or in a regular classroom. It can be conducted within the factory or in an outside training center in a public or a private proprietary school. The sponsors may be public authorities, individual employers, an association of employers, private schools, or even trade unions. The instruction may be academically oriented or given as a shop course.

There is in addition a wide range of programs that offer a combination of on-the-job and off-the-job training. Any type of training at work may require some course of related instruction given off the job. How the two are combined into a single training program varies considerably, depending upon the sponsoring organization.

The array of training methods can be arranged along a continuum, with off-the-job training at one extreme and on-the-job at the other, as illustrated by Figure 1. Training programs for the same skill can combine training both off and on the job in various mixes. Each curve indicates a specific number of trainees of equal quality; the higher the curve the larger the number of trainees. In the same way, these curves depict a successively higher quality of training of a fixed number of persons. The relative costs of training on and off the job yield a budget line that determines which particular mix of methods is most efficient, that is, the cheapest.

Training on the Job

In its broadest sense training on the job involves learning to perform certain tasks while performing on the production line. At the most basic level, a newly hired employee is first shown how to perform the simplest tasks at the work bench. When he succeeds with the easy tasks he is taught how to perform successively more complex operations. While this learning process is going on, the trainee is also working in the production process. To a large degree training on the job is a process of learning by doing.

More formal programs will have an instructor whose principal responsibility is to teach groups of trainees to perform a certain job in an efficient and safe manner. Depending on the level of skill the job requires, the training period may be quite short or it may extend a year or two. In numerous instances the program is self-paced so that each trainee learns as rapidly as he is able. In some of the less formal programs a supervisor may be responsible for conducting the training. But only in large firms with a substantial number of trainees would he spend a large amount of his time in training. In small plants where the number of trainees is also small, a fellow employee may be asked by management to show the new recruit how to do the job. In such situations the trainee learns a great deal by watching his co-workers.

Advantages. There are numerous advantages to the process of training on the job. For the trainee, the principal advantage is that he has a job and an income; he does not have to be concerned about finding a job after he completes his training. There is also a lesser chance of being trained for an obsolete skill. In many cases the trainee learns at his own speed and is therefore not pushed to maintain a difficult pace nor is he bored by repeating tasks already learned. Where jobs are arranged in a promotional hierarchy, on-the-job training in a helper-worker relationship becomes the process of upgrading. For the competent worker this offers the greatest opportunity for promotion.

From the company's point of view as well, training on the job has many advantages. In the context of the work environment it is possible to instill work habits which the company considers desirable, such as appropriate attitudes and shop discipline. It reduces the danger of training individuals to use obsolete methods and machinery because modern equipment and up-to-date trade practices are automatically available—though too expensive for training schools to keep up with. The worker is trained for a specific job with his employer, thus becoming valuable to the firm but not necessarily so to other companies. This cuts down on costly turnover, which is a distinct advantage to the firm that does the training.

Trainees on the job can make a positive contribution to output early in the training period, especially where a helper-journeyman relationship is customary and an essential part of the work assignment. Training on the job allows workers to keep abreast of current techniques, which is especially important in dynamic or rapidly evolving technologies.

Another distinct advantage of a training process which consists of showing or telling the trainee what to do is that the intellectual requirements of the trainee are minimal. He is not generally expected to read or write, except perhaps at a basic level, and his language or expressive ability can also be limited. Even where language barriers might inhibit normal conversation, a worker can be taught the job by being shown what to do and what not to do. In a shop situation the instructor can readily adapt his teaching to the capability and needs of the individual trainee. In addition the craftsman-instructor need not be schooled in pedagogy.

When specialized skills need to be taught to a small number of persons, there is no effective alternative to on-the-job training. Even one or two individuals can be placed in such a program without exorbitant cost.

From a social point of view there is a distinct financial advantage to training on the job instead of in public vocational schools. If development or industrialization is to some degree dependent upon enlarging the trained labor force, the government may decide to increase the capacity of the public vocational schools. This involves a direct cost to the government in public outlays for education. With on-the-job training the burden is shouldered by those directly affected: the firm and the individuals.

Disadvantages. To some degree, training on the job is disruptive to the production of a plant. While a trainee is learning, the machine he is using is not as fully productive as others. In addition a fellow worker or foreman is spending time away from his normal duties to give instruction, and this too is a cost to the firm. When the number of trainees is relatively small the amount of disruption to total output is also small, and the extra cost can be absorbed rather easily. With an increase in the number of trainees and the amount of time instructors spend away from their duties, however, the company's ability to absorb the costs diminishes. Training on the job is feasible only when the ratio of trainees to employees is small.

Training on the job has a relative advantage over vocational school training when the occupation to be taught requires only a low level of skill and hence a limited theoretical background. When an occupation demands theoretical knowledge, this cannot readily be imparted solely on the job and is best taught in a classroom situation.

Training at work presupposes the existence of job openings and often requires the individual to find his own job first, possibly without any information about the labor market or the guidance of someone able to provide occupational counseling. Training on the job also presupposes the existence of an industry, but this is not always the case in developing nations. Where the industry does not yet exist the training of manpower must of course be done outside the plant.

From society's point of view there are economic advantages to having craftsmen who are broadly rather than narrowly trained and thus have greater job mobility. Clearly, a broadly trained worker who becomes unemployed has more job opportunities than one who has only limited training. Workers who are trained on the job learn tasks and procedures peculiar to a single employer, which can be viewed as a disadvantage when it restricts their usefulness elsewhere. In addition to the difficulty of insuring that the trainee does not become overly specialized in the work process of a single shop, there is the problem of insuring that trainees are receiving instruction from skilled craftsmen who are also able to teach. The issue here is the uniform quality and breadth of training necessary to develop a complex skill sought by more than one employer.

In summary, on-the-job training without supplementary outside instruction is less than satisfactory under the following conditions: when a broadly trained worker is desired, when the work in a given firm is unique, when it is difficult for experienced workers to stop what they are doing and instruct a trainee, when it is difficult to transfer workers among different shops, or when the employer is reluctant to give the trainee varied work assignments.

Training off the Job

Training off the job may be offered in a shop class or a regular classroom. The former is used to provide practical experience needed for job training; the latter is used to teach general vocational knowledge.

Because of its broad approach, off-the-job training serves many purposes. It can impart vocational knowledge of immediate use at work, knowledge that must precede work, and knowledge that will be useful over the working life of the individual but is not needed immediately. It can also refresh or sharpen academic skills, such as arithmetic and reading, or related instruction such as shop theory. It can also provide vocational skills that are not taught on the job because it is technically impractical to do so or too expensive because of the production time that is lost in training.

Training off the job can take place in a variety of settings: public vocational schools, companies, and private schools.

Public vocational schools. The public vocational school normally is part of the regular public school system. In many countries students are assigned to a vocational or a college preparatory school on the basis of examinations. Those who do not qualify for the academic are assigned to the vocational program. In other countries the selection is left to the students, but with advice from guidance counselors. Where the vocational program has a good reputation, students who are manually oriented will make a positive choice; elsewhere it is sometimes used as a dumping ground for the less qualified academic students. In most cases there are no tuition costs to the students.

The average public vocational school offers training in a number of basic fields such as woodworking, machine shop, electrical work, and auto repair. After some orientation in the various types of work, a student selects an area in which to specialize, though his choice may be limited by the predetermined size of the class. Once the selection is made the student spends a substantial amount of his school time learning about and performing on the specialized equipment in the shop. In addition he takes courses related to his specialty, such as shop math and blueprint reading. In many countries, especially where the vocational students are so young that they have not completed their basic education, the program also offers general courses, such as history, literature, and grammar. Vocational school programs usually run for about three years, but this varies. As part of the public school system, they are administered by the Ministry of Education. Instructors are therefore governed by the general civil service rules, but the requirements for teaching shop classes normally include some years of experience in the trade. Depending on the size of the program, the physical facilities may or may not be independent of other parts of the school system. A small program, for example, may be administered as part of a large secondary school where vocational and academic students participate jointly in some courses. It should be noted that the facilities can be used after school, on weekends, and in the evenings for adult vocational training.

In companies. Training off the job may be provided in a firm's own facilities apart from the production process. Depending on the size of the program, it may be conducted in a special room in the plant or in a separate building on the firm's property. Normally students in such a program are assured of a job with the company upon successful completion of the course. The basic shop courses train workers in the use of the firm's equipment, although related instruction may also be offered if it is relevant to the skill required. A large company may set up equipment in a shop class where the trainees get all their experience; other companies may use their regular production equipment for training but at a time when little or no disruption to output occurs.

Skill centers. A skill or training center offers training in one or more skills to persons who have finished their legally required schooling, either by graduating or dropping out. It may be sponsored by a government agency or, frequently, a group of employers or an industrial association. In addition to shop classes a training center offers related instruction, but academic courses are unlikely. If sponsored by a government agency, the center probably offers programs for occupations that are generally considered in short supply, and the trainees are apt to be broadly trained to meet the needs of a variety of firms and industries. If the center is sponsored by an industrial group, however, it is likely to offer programs for occupations specifically needed by the industry, and the trainees will receive rather narrow training. An industrial group would be more apt to finance and sponsor a training center when the average firm in the industry is not large enough to support its own in-plant program.

Private schools. The private proprietary school is a profit-making organization that establishes training programs for occupations that seem to be in great demand and are likely to continue growing. Generally the courses are geared to students who have completed the legally required years of schooling, and training is limited to a few areas. The facilities include classrooms where related instruction is offered and shops which normally contain rather simple or obsolete machinery. It is assumed that with a broad exposure to a trade, a reasonably able graduate would learn to handle any new machine after a short time on the job. Courses are offered both day and evening, and the tuition charges are generally rather high.

Advantages. Off-the-job training assumes that trainees require a certain amount of vocational or technical knowledge before entering the plant or shop or being assigned specific work tasks. Preliminary instruction is deemed necessary to prevent injury to the trainee, damage to equipment, or waste of materials. It also prepares the worker for the additional training he may get on the job. In short the individual cannot perform safely or be instructed with reasonable effectiveness or at reasonable cost without some initial familiarity with the work process and work procedures and an understanding of the terminology used in the trade.

Training off the job, alone or in conjunction with on-the-job training, is appropriate for the more complex skills which require preliminary training before the trainee actively performs on the job. It produces a broadly trained individual who can apply his skill in a variety of work situations or establishments and is able to meet problems with discretion as they arise. The skills are usually based on a relatively organized, systematic body of theory that is best presented formally in class. Such broad training offers the individual who completes the program greater mobility and the possibility of finding a job in several industries.

The public vocational school generally has the advantage of being able to offer general academic courses in addition to vocational training. In many countries youths engaged in vocational programs have not completed their general education; in some cases this means they have not learned to read and write sufficiently well to profit from their training. The dual offerings of public vocational schools makes it possible for these youths to take vocational courses along with the necessary academic work. Furthermore the programs can be generalized beyond the confines of particular traditional skills so that a young worker learns more than one trade. The same basic training is now used for many different trades, with specialization only toward the end of the program.

In contrast to on-the-job programs which are limited to a relatively small number of trainees because of the costs involved, off-the-job training programs can handle larger numbers. In addition, a single employer may lack the technical know-how to direct training and probably would find it uneconomical to employ training specialists. An off-the-job training center has none of these disadvantages. The center need not be a public one but can be operated and financed by an employer association. Such an arrangement captures the advantages of training by specialists as well as the low unit cost of institutional instruction.

Off-the-job training programs are likely to be able to offer courses at all times during the day and week on both a full-time and part-time basis. This flexibility invites widespread participation whether by youths interested in a full-time program or working adults who want an evening course.

Disadvantages. An obvious disadvantage to training off the job is that there are certain minimal requirements for successful training at reasonable costs: Trainees must be literate, probably not below a sixth grade level, and have commensurate proficiency in computational skills; they must share a common language to facilitate group presentation of materials. In addition there must be enough students in each class to make economical use of the investment in facilities and equipment. When the size and location of firms or the characteristics of the local labor force results in a small number of students, training off the job, otherwise desirable, may be extremely expensive per trainee.

Unlike training at work, training off the job requires instructors who are both skilled craftsmen and schooled in pedagogy and who might be alternatively employed in production or supervisory work. An instructor's time might be underutilized if he is solely a classroom or shop teacher, but training on the job allows him to teach and work simultaneously or devote part of his work day to teaching and the remainder to production or supervisory activities. There is an obvious cost advantage to this dual role when the instructor would not otherwise be fully utilized. Furthermore, training off the job requires additional personnel to teach skilled craftsmen the techniques and theory of pedagogy they need to become effective vocational teachers.

There is a possibility that public vocational schooling might encourage an individual to continue his education and thus divert him from entering the trade for which he has been trained. This would be particularly apt to happen if the vocational school is seen as a substitute for high school and a step toward a technical or engineering degree or a white-collar job. For private proprietary schools a drawback is that the direct cost of tuition is so high that low-income families are excluded from participating. Private schools become a realistic alternative only where the free training programs are either filled to capacity or offering obviously inferior training. Furthermore, resources devoted to job development and placement add to the cost of school programs.

Frequently on-the-job training programs have been developed because traditional systems of vocational preparation in public or private schools did not meet the needs of modern industry. Vocational school programs are often too theoretical and not job related, and graduates are not ready to enter the production process. Training programs off the job have a tendency to become inflexible, especially when the school has obligations to teaching staff and where expensive equipment has been purchased. In addition school programs bear the burden of the extra cost of revising curricula to adapt to changing techniques and developing resources for job placement.

A final disadvantage for graduates of off-the-job training is the necessity of finding a job after the program is completed. Although the whole program is geared to learning a trade and working at it, all graduates do not find work in the trade for which they are trained, and many spend long periods looking for a job. This is an economic waste from society's point of view.

Combined Types of Training

A number of programs combine some aspects of on-the-job and off-the-job training, but there are three basic types: apprenticeship, training on the job plus related instruction, and cooperative-work training and sandwich courses.

Apprenticeship. This is a formal program of a predetermined duration which varies with each trade. It combines training at work with formal, mandatory related instruction conducted in the classroom or shop class off the job. There is a prescribed curriculum to be taught in a coherent order with an explicit obligation by the employer to provide training in the tasks necessary to produce a well-rounded journeyman. The employer implicitly commits himself to employ the apprentice when his training is completed. The successful trainee receives a certificate that can be used much like a high school diploma or college degree as evidence that he has attained a certain proficiency in his trade. In a number of countries (the United States and Canada are prime examples), apprenticeships are generally limited to a relatively small number of skilled crafts referred to as apprenticeable trades. These include the skilled occupations in construction, printing, and machinery. In most other countries around the world the apprenticeship type of training includes not only skilled crafts but also many semiskilled as well as white-collar occupations. Usually the programs are supported and developed by employers or employer associations, although there is frequent support by both the government and the trade unions.

In many Western European countries related classes are often held during scheduled work hours. The apprentices are on released time with pay and thus receive their training on and off the job during the regular work day with compensation for the total time. In the United States, however, the common practice is for apprentices to get related instruction on their own time, usually outside working hours in the evening, although Saturday morning classes are not uncommon.

Training on the job plus related instruction. This type of program combines some related instruction, given off the job, with a specific form of training on the job. Many on-the-job programs, because of the nature of the training or the skills needed for the occupation, require or strongly urge trainees to take specific related courses. In most cases the trainees take such courses on their own time and frequently pay the tuition out of their own funds. In other on-the-job programs it is recommended or suggested that trainees take some related instruction, but such course work is not integrated with the training on the job and is used only as a broadening element in the development of the workers.

Cooperative work training and sandwich courses. With young trainees whose formal education is still incomplete, mandatory classroom attendance in public schools combined with training on the job is known as cooperative work training. The trainee is still a student and spends more time in the classroom than do adult workers because he must take academic subjects required for a high school diploma. Such programs involve the cooperation of school and employer inasmuch as the trainee spends part of each day, week, or even month in school and the remaining time at work where he receives training, frequently with pay. The schoolwork is not entirely academic but includes shop courses and related instruction in the area of the trainee's occupational interest.

Sandwich courses are a common variation of cooperative work training whereby an adult with a regular full-time job is given time off from work to take vocational courses. They may be geared to a specific trade or job or to upgrading, but in either case they provide additional training to workers who could not afford to give up their jobs or lose time for this instruction. Generally the cost of sandwich courses is borne by the employer.

Advantages. Because of the diverse combinations of training on and off the job, the advantages of one need not apply to another. Apprenticeship, for example, has the advantage of being generally recognized as the official training program by employers, public authorities, and trade unions. An apprentice who successfully completes the program receives a certificate which in many countries confers top priority in the competition for jobs. The holder of such a certificate is assumed to have acquired the necessary skill and technique to perform his trade adequately with little or no extra training on the job. Many countries have instituted a test of competence at the end of the apprenticeship period which is conducted by an independent authority and leads to a nationally recognized credential.

Where theoretical aspects of an occupation are critical to the skill but cannot be taught economically on the job, there is no alternative but to combine on-the-job and off-the-job training. For highly skilled crafts that require knowledge of an organized body of theory, training on the job by itself, without related instruction, probably lengthens the training period or produces a worker with more limited skills.

In general, the major arguments for or against training only on the job depend on the breadth of training that is desired. The discussion centers on the variety of tasks that a worker can expect to encounter on any one job or in any one shop while practicing his craft. If the work in a given shop is highly specialized, but it is desirable to produce a broadly trained worker, vocational school courses might supplement the work experience and acquaint trainees with tasks and situations they are unlikely to meet with a single employer. To train a versatile worker who is capable of performing many different tasks for a variety of employers with disparate requirements, it is essential to combine instruction on the job with classroom courses off the job. With on-the-job training alone the individual would have to rotate among employers to gain the maximum exposure to the work of his trade. Such rotation can be difficult if not impossible to implement, however, and the trainee may still not encounter the full range of experiences desired. Depending on the relative growth potential of different industries and/or different firms within the same industry, a highly mobile, skilled work force may be desirable, in which case a certain amount of related instruction in a classroom situation would be required.

When young people enter the labor force before becoming fully literate, a combination of classroom instruction and training on the job might curb their tendency to cut short their education. There is some indication that such a combination (especially where the trainee receives wages during his on-the-job training) has deterred potential school dropouts.

Disadvantages. The drawbacks of one combination of on-the-job and off-the-job training, like its merits, cannot be applied to another. For example, a basic disadvantage to apprenticeship is the tendency for the program to have a longer duration than appears necessary in terms of the theoretical and technical knowledge required for skilled crafts. An argument in defense of its long duration is that it is necessary to enable an adolescent to adapt himself to work in a factory and to the physiological and emotional problems

associated with this stage of life. Another disadvantage is the
unions use the apprentice system to limit the supply of skil
Where a significant percentage of journeymen learn their ti
route, controlling entrance to the training program effectively limits the
number of skilled craftsmen.

Cooperative programs require good coordination between schools and industry and intense supervision to insure that trainees are not merely rele-
gated to menial tasks. But this level of coordination and supervision is very
difficult to achieve. In addition cooperative programs require the assurance
that relevant jobs will be available to participants throughout the period of
the program. Because of the vagaries of the labor market, however, administrators are not always able to give assurances of this kind.

3

Factors Affecting the Selection of a Training Mode

The choice of training workers on the job, off the job, or with some combination of the two rests ultimately on economic and institutional factors. Among economic factors are the cost of training, the urgency with which the skilled workers are needed, and in the case of training in companies the profitability of training to the enterprise. Institutional factors include the existing training environment, training laws, the influence of unions and employer associations, attitudes of employers, and the nature of the labor market.

ECONOMIC FACTORS

If it is assumed that the output of the training process is the same whether it is located in a school or in a plant, the choice will depend on the relative average cost of training. The average training cost of a program is influenced to a large extent by the number of trainees, the relationship of the program to other training programs in the same institution, and the nature of the laboratories and instruction needed.

Size of the Program

A given scale of operation is determined by the fixed size of the plant or instructional staff. For this scale there is usually a cost per student or unit of training which is lower than all other unit costs. This is sometimes referred to as the optimum unit cost for a given plant size and in microeconomics is usually represented by a U-shaped average cost curve.

Figure 2. Comparison of Average Costs of Training in Plant and in School

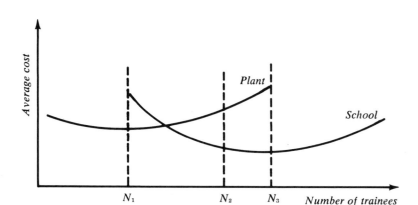

This curve assumes the shape of a U for the relatively simple reason that for small quantities average costs are high because fixed costs are spread out over only a few units. As the quantity increases, fixed costs are spread out over more units; in addition, variable factors can be used more efficiently relative to the fixed ones and relative to each other, and the average cost will therefore decrease. After the minimum average cost is reached, variable factors cannot be used as efficiently as before, and the advantage of lower average fixed cost is outweighed by the increase of average variable cost.

Every scale of operation can theoretically produce a particular number of trainees at a lowest possible average cost. To compare average costs of training in two different settings, school and industry, it is first necessary to specify whether the comparison is to find out which mode of training is cheaper for a given number of trainees or which mode can provide the lowest average cost of training for an unspecified number of trainees. The problem is illustrated in Figure 2. At N_1 training in plant is less costly; at N_2 training in school is more advantageous. But the lowest possible average cost of training could be achieved only if N_3 could be trained in school.

Existence of Other Training Programs

It is sometimes possible to lower the average cost of training of a particular program by increasing the enrollment in related programs which share common resources or by adding new programs that can take advantage of existing resources. For example, training only twenty students in an oxyacetylene welding program will result in a high average cost if this enrollment level utilizes only 50 percent of the time of a welding instructor and laboratory. But it is possible to increase utilization of the available capacity

Figure 3. Average Costs in Type A Laboratory

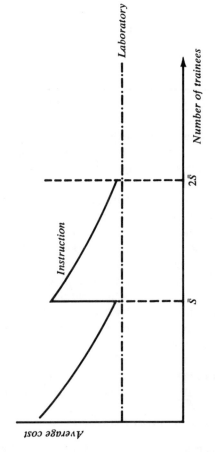

and hence lower laboratory cost per trainee by adding twenty students in arc welding or by increasing the enrollment in sheet metal and machine shops, each of which requires some instruction in welding.

Of course, a decision to expand enrollment has to be based on the way in which marginal cost is affected by the larger enrollment in the programs and the increased utilization of capacity for oxyacetylene welding. But the increase or decrease in marginal cost is difficult to assess because most programs share resources in different proportions. For example, training in sheet metal skills requires the following weekly hours of instruction:

Course	Hours	Stations[1]
Sheet metal	18	0.60
Welding	6	0.20
Mathematics	2	0.06
Drafting	4	0.14

In order to increase the utilization of welding by two stations, ten more students would have to be enrolled in the sheet metal program. But ten more students in the sheet metal program will require six more stations in sheet metal instruction. This may exceed the existing capacity[2] of the sheet metal laboratory. Therefore the need to train more sheet metal workers must be determined as well as the cost of expanding the laboratory for sheet metal instruction if no excess capacity is available.

Nature of the Laboratories

The size of many laboratories and instructional staffs cannot be increased in a continuous fashion by the addition of individual learning stations or machines where a number of students can learn at one time. Instead whole units or groups of machines must be added. Thus a single lathe added to a machine shop will allow an increased enrollment in the training of machine lathe operators, but another laboratory such as for auto mechanics will require several different machines in a given proportion to train only a few additional students.

1. A station is one student instructional site used thirty hours a week.
2. Laboratory capacity is defined by the queuing capacity of the machinery and sometimes varies with the locale. In the United States, for instance, a lathe would be considered a single instructional station and scheduled accordingly, but in European countries it is not uncommon for two, three, or even four students to be working on a lathe at the same time. Because laboratories require at least 15 percent unused capacity to allow flexibility in scheduling and station loading, an optimal utilization is around 85 percent.

Figure 4. Average Costs in Type B Laboratory at Capacity

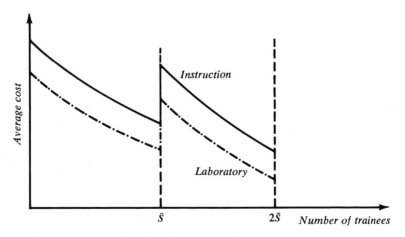

$\bar{S} =$ Optimum number of students per teacher

Figure 5. Average Costs in Type B Laboratory with Excess Capacity

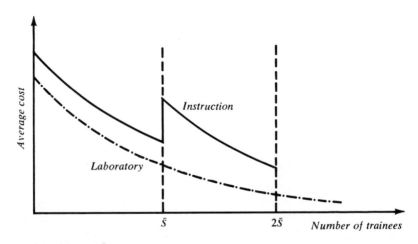

$\bar{S} =$ Optimum number of students per teacher

In general, it is possible to classify laboratories into two types: Type A contains one or only a few types of machines necessary to train for a specific occupation, and the number of machines varies linearly with the number of students. In this type of laboratory the cost per student will vary with the use of the instructional capacity. Average costs in this type of laboratory are represented in Figure 3.

Type B laboratories require a configuration of equipment. For example, a minimum laboratory for auto mechanics would need an engine analyzer, wheel alignment system, electrical equipment, and so on. The average cost varies with the number of trainees as shown in Figures 4 and 5. In Figure 4 the minimum size of the laboratory corresponds to the optimum student-teacher ratio. In Figure 5 the capacity of the laboratory exceeds the optimum student-teacher ratio.

In view of the intricate relationship among curricula of different training programs and the varied characteristics of laboratories, the problem of maximizing the utilization of resources can be met only through the use of complicated optimizing models. It may be unnecessary and even undesirable to maximize utilization, however, if the school is to be flexible in its offerings over time. Once a school reaches a moderate size in staff and equipment, a utilization of 80 to 85 percent of capacity is sufficient and will accommodate minor changes in enrollment levels or the addition of a small number of new programs. In some developed countries it is felt that an enrollment of 500 to 750 students will provide flexibility and good utilization of capacity, depending of course on the nature of the program. It is generally possible to get an adequate solution with relatively easy calculations. See Appendix A for an example of how to calculate the costs of a training program.

The Time Factor

When there is no urgent need for trained workers, the relative cost of training becomes the principal factor in determining the selection of the training method. When the need is urgent, however, the principal factor is the comparative speed of training. If a plant cannot operate efficiently because it lacks skilled workers, the choice of a cheaper but longer training mode would be a case of suboptimization—optimizing a part of the system and not the whole system. The correct course of action would be to choose a faster, even though costlier, method of training as long as the increase in the cost of training is smaller than the cost of an inefficient plant operation for a longer period of time.

Figure 6 shows a continuous spectrum of modes of training, represented by lines $T_1, T_2, \ldots T_n$, and budget lines marked $B_1, B_2, \ldots B_n$. The points $A_1, A_2, \ldots A_n$ are the modes of training that minimize the cost of training. Points $C_1, C_2, \ldots C_n$ represent modes that minimize the time needed (the

Figure 6. Training Modes That Minimize Costs Compared with Those That Minimize Training Time

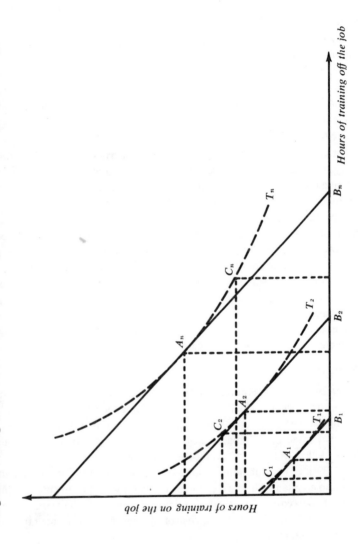

sum of hours of on- and off-the-job training) but are more expensive than modes $A_1, A_2, \ldots A_n$. However, as long as the difference between the cost of C and A is less than the cost of lower efficiency in the plant over a longer training period, the modes represented by C should be chosen.

The time factor in training is especially important when staffing a new plant or industry. With the press of problems at the beginning of operation, there is usually little or no time for the careful training of inexperienced employees and good reason for off-the-job training. Often a plant or industry will fill its initial need for trained or semitrained workers by hiring them away from other domestic companies which employ the same or similar skills. Two questions for government policymakers are: How critical are the trained workers to the establishments that will lose them? And, if recruitment requires raising wages, how will this affect wage and price relationships?

One alternative solution to the staffing problem is to recruit foreign personnel on a temporary basis. A second is for companies which are losing personnel to the newer firms to start an upgrading program in their own plants and hire unskilled workers at the bottom. A third alternative to pirating skilled workers from other domestic companies is for the new firm to establish a training program before starting production. Some experiments have already proved successful in this area. Normally many months pass between the time equipment is installed and the start-up of production. This time could be used for intensive training of skilled workers. Foreign technicians might be brought in as instructors, or in some cases representatives of the equipment manufacturers could be used as a resource for training workers.

PROFITABILITY TO THE FIRM OF IN-PLANT TRAINING

The relative cost of training is only one factor in deciding the advantage of a mode of training. When training in private enterprise is contemplated, its profitability to the enterprise has to be considered. Employers will invest in training if the expected return will equal or exceed the cost of training. The equilibrium equation for training a worker in a plant can be written as follows:

$$\sum_{t=1}^{m} \frac{C_t + W_{at} - Q_{at}}{(1+r)^t} = \sum_{t=m+1}^{n} \frac{Q_{st} - W_{st}}{(1+r)^t}$$

where C_t = cost of training a worker over a unit of time t
W_{at} = wage rate of trainee during t
Q_{at} = value of production attributable to a trainee during t

W_{st} = wage rate of a skilled worker during t
Q_{st} = value of production attributable to a skilled worker during t
r = rate of discount for the firm
t = time subscript
m = length of training period
n = length of time the skilled worker remains in the firm.

These variables are discussed below.

Cost of In-plant Training

The decision to offer training in the plant depends to a large extent on the cost of training and trainees' wages. Included in the total training cost are the cost of initiating and administering the training program, capital costs, supplies and materials, fixed and variable costs of instruction, training fees, miscellaneous, and other.[3] The cost of initiating training covers the setting up of the program by the designated authority, whether this is someone already employed in the factory, outside consultants, people especially hired to perform this function, or some combination of initiators. When the program is set up in-house it is difficult to determine the actual cost, especially when the people involved may be performing many other functions at the same time. Some criteria must be developed for assigning these joint costs to the training program. The cost of initiating the program should be considered a fixed cost and allocated over the life of the training program. Later changes that update the program and have effect for a long time should be considered in the same vein.

The cost of administering the program includes the salaries of administrators, the prorated cost of office equipment and materials, the cost of selection and recruitment including advertising for vacancies, school visits, interviewing and testing, and follow-up of trainees in the factory.

The capital costs for training include the cost of land, buildings, and equipment used and are allocated over the life of the program. Special care must be taken to employ the correct methods for figuring depreciation and allocating costs when the equipment or buildings are used also for production. Materials and supplies are variable and consumable costs that are related to capital costs.

The fixed cost of instruction includes the preparation of teaching materials and the training of teaching staff. This should also be allocated over the life of the training program. The variable cost of instruction is the

---

3. This list is based on "A Cost-Benefit Analysis of Industrial Training" by Brinkly Thomas, John Maxham, and J.A.G. Jones, *British Journal of Industrial Relations*, Vol. VII, No. 2, and on "A Standard Method of Costing: The Training of Apprentices," *Bacie Journal*, September 1960.

actual cost of instructors especially hired for training or the imputed value of the teaching services of plant personnel engaged mainly in the production process but whose duties also include instruction.

When the firm sends its trainees to take courses or be trained in programs provided by other institutions, sometimes it pays for the courses. Fees paid by the firm for outside courses should be included in the total cost of training.

Miscellaneous costs include a variety of items such as statutory and social costs—payment for holidays, insurance, contribution to pension schemes, subsidization of meals, travel, and accommodation. Included under other costs are those that cannot be directly assigned to training. These are related to the increase in the probability of damaging equipment, spoiling production, and interfering with the normal operations of the plant.

Valuation of Partial Services of Employees and Capital

When staff is hired and equipment purchased specifically for training, the allocation of expense is relatively simple. To evaluate the training services of people and equipment whose main purpose in a plant is production is not an easy task, however. In accordance with strict economic theory only the opportunity costs of existing resources should be taken into account. But what is the opportunity cost of the short time a skilled worker spends teaching a trainee? The fact that his time is available or a machine is idle should not be construed as indicating that the opportunity cost is zero. Each production establishment needs a certain amount of flexibility in its scheduling and therefore requires a certain amount of unemployed resources to function properly. If the added demands of training result in the full use of resources, this may introduce inefficiency. However, any unused capacity of machinery and skills beyond the amount of freedom needed for flexibility of operations can be considered a resource with a low opportunity cost. (It is seldom zero.) Here the problem of the size of the training program is important—the smaller program is more likely to take advantage of available resources with low opportunity costs. The larger program is less able to do this, but it has a greater chance of achieving economies of scale through structured instruction.

Wage rates of trainees. The level of wages paid to trainees affects the profitability of training to the firm: The lower the wages, the more profitable the training. There is, however, a minimal limit for wages that the firm must exceed in order to entice trainees into the program. This limit is largely determined by the opportunity costs of the trainees' time.

The value of trainees' production. When trainees are segregated from the regular production workers, the valuation of production is straightforward: (1) the percentage of the trainee's time that is spent on production is calculated; (2) the trainee's level of productivity in proportion to that of a skilled worker's productivity is computed; (3) finally, the total value of production for the firm is the product of (1) and (2) multiplied by the wage of a skilled worker. The value of production of a trainee working in a team with skilled workers can be determined only when it is possible to substitute trainees for skilled workers and measure the difference in the team's production with and without the trainee.

Wage rate of a skilled worker. In a competitive market for trained workers wages equal the marginal product minus the cost of labor turnover. A worker who quits produces a loss to the firm in the form of the cost of hiring a replacement and the initial lower level of productivity before the newly hired worker becomes acquainted with the machinery and environment. Many times a firm will offer training with the hope of minimizing labor turnover. In this case in-house training is intended to make withdrawal from the firm more costly to the worker because of his own investment in some specific training, in social relationships, and in his adaptation to the work environment.

In a competitive market a firm will be willing to offer training only if the benefit from lowering the turnover rate is large or there is a possibility of recouping the cost of training during the training period. This possibility will be enhanced if the trainee can be paid wages below the value of his production and if the apprenticeship period can be lengthened and a legal restraint put on deserting the firm before completion of the contract. The market in which a firm hires its labor is not competitive when the workers have training that is specific to the firm or in the case of monopsony when the firm is the sole employer for a segment of the labor market. Under such noncompetitive conditions wages are always lower than marginal productivity, although they are largely dependent on the bargaining power of the workers in the specific occupation. Everything else being equal, there is therefore a greater probability that a firm would offer training when the labor market is noncompetitive.

Elements that Favor Training in the Firm

Noneconomic behavior and imperfections in the labor market contribute to the feasibility of training in the firm. As explained above, the lack of competition is one market imperfection. Another is a level of unemployment high enough to limit mobility and induce employees to settle for wages lower than they might obtain elsewhere. Fragmentation of the labor market also hampers mobility between different occupations. Insufficient market information induces workers to accept wages that are lower by at least the amount it would cost to acquire the needed information. Noneconomic motivations that may prompt a business to finance training include a desire to make a philanthropic contribution, achieve a political goal, or generate good will. The fidelity of workers to the firm is another form of non-economic behavior that induces them to accept lower wages during and after training thereby making training more profitable to the firm.

Economic Policies to Encourage Training in Industry

On the basis of the above economic variables that affect profitability of training in industry, it is possible to design policies to induce firms to undertake training. When training is firm-specific it will probably take place in the firm without public support unless the cost of training is very high. Because of their nature, some types of training may not be justified on economic grounds alone but only in terms of broader goals. In other cases the size of the firm does not allow economies of scale in training.

When costs are high because of the small scale of operations, there is a rationale for providing the administrative machinery to develop an efficient scale of training. This administrative machinery may have to be financed with public funds. When economies of scale can be achieved through a cooperative program sponsored by an industry or group of industries, however, there is no rationale for subsidizing training specific to a firm; nor is there any justification for subsidizing a monopsonistic industry. For cross-industry occupations (those commonly found in different industries) there is a case for subsidizing the cost of training and/or wages paid to the trainee in order to attract him to the program.

If there is a competitive market for skilled labor, public authorities may introduce laws that compel a trainee to remain with the firm that trained him for a certain time after he reaches proficiency in the occupation but before being classified as a skilled worker. This period could be long enough to allow the firm to recoup the costs of training. For this system to be effective, firms that hire away workers who did not fulfill their contract must reimburse the firm that trained them for part of the training costs. This type of legal imposition on the trainee must be used carefully to avoid exploitation of workers at substandard wages.

Because the benefits of training do not accrue to the firm until long after the program is set up, a low discount rate on loans for training programs would encourage firms to establish them. Public authorities can provide loans at interest lower than commercial rates. These loans could be managed and controlled more easily by assigning them for the purchase of machinery, equipment, and materials specific for training, and/or the construction of special buildings for in-plant schooling.

Tax incentives. Besides direct intervention in the form of subsidies and loans at low interest rates, public authorities may encourage training in enterprises by allowing the firm to deduct training costs from its accrued taxes.

A common procedure is to consider training as an expense. The actual cost of training for the firm is thus its outlay multiplied by one minus the income tax rate. For example, if the tax rate is 50 percent the cost to the firm is only half the actual outlay. This type of education has the disadvantage of making training a function of profits rather than of needs.

Whenever there is a levy on training in the form of a payroll tax or value-added tax, there is usually a provision to reimburse firms for the training done in their plants. As long as reimbursements exceed training costs minus benefits, there is an economic gain to the firm engaged in training.

It has been suggested also that an ad valorem tax be imposed on imported machinery and the proceeds used for training. Such a tax can be justified on the grounds that training is a necessary adjunct to the equipment and therefore the users of capital goods should bear the burden of the complementary training. In addition, in developing countries where there is an acute unemployment problem, a tax on imported capital is consonant with a policy that tries to make capital more expensive relative to labor. When establishing a training-import tax, provision can be made for firms to deduct training costs from this tax. This provides incentives for the firm to undertake training up to a cost equivalent to the amount of the tax.

All of these incentives discriminate against small firms which in many instances cannot take advantage of tax deductions because they do not employ enough trainees to have even minimum-size classes needed for courses. Larger firms can of course organize full courses for many different skills, including the upgrading of management. Tax deductions for training costs therefore benefit firms that would have been training their own personnel in any case, especially when jobs are specific to an industry or the industry is the only employer.

There are two basic corrective measures. One is the application of a graduated tax. A payroll tax based on a firm's size, for instance, would tax smaller firms proportionately less and solve the inequity of the tax burden. A second and more important measure is the creation of an administrative structure with public funds to encourage training cooperatives to achieve economies of scale and greater efficiency.

Nonmonetary incentives. To encourage in-plant training programs, public facilities might be made available for use by private firms. A major cost of training is the production of didactic materials and pedagogic guidance, which could also be supplied to an interested firm. Public authorities could further lessen the cost of training by providing teachers of general subjects, testing students, and offering other ancillary services.

Incentives to in-plant training beyond the firm's training needs. The amount of training a firm can offer is limited by its future requirements as to the size and characteristics of its labor force. If the public authorities wish to encourage a firm to take in more trainees than its limit allows, the cost of training the extra numbers will have to be covered. If the firm is repaid its average costs, such an arrangement will be profitable to the firm only when average costs are higher than marginal costs.

INSTITUTIONAL CONSIDERATIONS

In addition to the purely economic factors there are some institutional elements that influence the choice of a mode of training: the character of the labor market, the attitudes of industry and unions toward certain methods, the power of the vocational school lobby, and the availability of curricula, vocational teachers, and administrators.

The Character of the Labor Market

The major aspects of the labor market that merit consideration in choosing a mode of training are: entry requirements of jobs, wages, unemployment, channels of labor market information, and the government as employer.

Entry requirement of jobs. A very important part of the hiring process is the general entry requirements for new employees. In certain industries union membership is a prerequisite for a job. In theory, this is based on the notion that union membership assures that the worker has a certain level of competence. Actually, however, the practice may be no more than an indication of the monopolistic position of the union. Other hiring-in qualifications may include a primary school or a secondary school diploma or a certificate indicating completion of an apprenticeship or a vocational school program. Some firms are prepared to hire untrained persons with a certain minimum level of schooling if the person agrees to enter the firm's training program. Continued employment is then dependent upon successful progress in the training program.

Jobs above the entry level may require specific years of experience. If a firm follows the practice of promotion from within, then almost all new hiring will be for jobs at the lowest paid, least skilled, entry level. If a firm hires at all levels then obviously job experience will be required for some, but the qualifications vary from industry to industry, and from firm to firm.

When entry requirements for new employees are relatively high and also rigid, especially when educational levels are specified, then training in a school situation, off the job, is more appropriate. In the schools, trainees with deficiencies in general education can take special courses to attain the required minimum level.

Wages. In any single industry what are the differences between the wages of the skilled, semiskilled, and unskilled workers? What are the differences between two industries for the same skill level? What is the difference in wage between a skilled craftsman and a vocational instructor of the same craft?

In an industry where wage rates are relatively high, training on the job becomes expensive. Not only are the wages of the trainees rather high, but also the cost of the production time lost by journeymen when they are giving instruction. In this case training off the job, especially in the classroom, could be considerably cheaper.

When the wage structure of an industry is compressed and the difference between the unskilled and skilled workers is small, there may be little incentive among employees to train for a higher level. In such a situation it may be preferable to offer the training off the job. If the difference between unskilled and skilled is wide, however, there would be a strong incentive to enter an on-the-job training program.

Unemployment. When unemployment is relatively high, training on the job is clearly preferable because it generally assures the trainee a job if he completes the program successfully. Other modes of training simply provide the graduate with a license to search for a job, an intolerable situation if unemployment is already high. When unemployment is high the opportunity cost of students is much lower, however, which is a point in favor of the formal educational setting.

Channels of labor market information. How employers broadcast the news about available jobs and how workers hear about these vacancies affects not only the response to different modes of training but also the placement of graduates. If word of mouth is the basic channel of information about jobs then facts about on-the-job training are more likely to be disseminated throughout the area and in-school training is not likely to receive enough publicity to attract large numbers of qualified applicants. Labor exchange bureaus which process large numbers of job seekers offer a more systematic avenue of communication and easily disseminate all types of relevant information about training.

In some industries trade unions are a principal source of news about job vacancies. Sometimes the unions may actually make the placement or union membership may be a minimum requirement for the job. Agreements between trade unions and employers on hiring practices may be formal or informal, but in either case they favor training under the auspices of unions and employers.

In some countries it is not uncommon for the government, through one or more of its agencies, to provide vocational placement services free of charge. Information is provided about projected needs of various occupations, the salaries paid, and the kind of training needed to become a craftsman in that occupation. Often such information is directed to young people at a critical point in their educational career to help them select wisely according to the needs of the labor market. If vocational placement services are common, the government could also use them to publicize the various training programs available.

Government as employer. In developing nations the government is often a major employer of trained manpower and has the opportunity to plan the whole process of training for the specific jobs needed; it operates both the public schools and the plants. Such a monopolistic position in the labor market permits the government to select the better employees and the best means of training.

Attitude of Industry and Unions

The economic environment and the experience of the industry will determine the beliefs and opinions that firms hold about various training programs. In most cases their bias will focus on a specific type of training such as public vocational schools, industry-wide skill centers, or in-plant training. If, for example, industry in general is prejudiced against public vocational schools there would seem to be little merit in expanding training in the public school system regardless of other factors.

Often firms within an industry form an employer association to engage in mutually beneficial activities. When there are labor shortages such associations will act to protect its members from outside competition in the labor market. One protective measure is the establishment of a skill center to train workers for the specific and specialized needs of the industry. Such narrowly trained workers do not then have the necessary skills to move to jobs in other industries. By supporting a skill center an employer association is thus indirectly tying the trained workers to the industry. Employer associations could also help develop cooperative training programs that involve classroom instruction in the public schools and on-the-job training in the member firms of the association.

The existence of a strong labor union may make it difficult to initiate an on-the-job training program. Problems such as the wage rates for trainees and the ratio of trainees to journeymen may result in delays and an ineffective program. Under these circumstances it may be preferable to use an off-the-job program in a school setting.

The Power of the Vocational School Lobby

Vocational schools are more in the public eye than any other training program in a country. The relationship of vocational school personnel to other groups in the community is significant for the overall acceptance of vocational training. If vocational school personnel have a good relationship with the ministry of labor and the ministry of education, then substantial funds will be made available to vocational training programs; the reverse is also true. Lobbying is an acceptable pattern of behavior, and if the vocational school lobby has muscle many of its programs will receive political support. If vocational school teachers or directors are organized into associations, their political and economic leverage will be high.

The relations between vocational school personnel and the leaders of the business community are also important. If the relationship is good, firms are more likely to employ vocational school graduates; and favorable prospects for jobs will in turn generate interest among youths in gaining entrance to the vocational schools.

Availability of Curricula, Vocational Teachers, and Administrators

Critical to all types of formal training programs is the availability of curricula. If any formal training is offered in the country then some curricula are available, and information on them can be readily obtained from the school system and some of the large employers. These existing programs can often be expanded or used as models for new programs. Curricula for in-school training, for example, might be adapted for use in training centers and on-the-job programs. Curricula can also be imported, but they are not likely to be usable without considerable modification. Without some sort of curriculum to use as a model, however, it would be almost impossible to start a program with any semblance of logical progression. Following the standard pattern of work in a shop, a foreman or trainer would have to show how various tasks are performed, and a trainee could learn by watching and doing.

Although scarcities of vocational teachers may be overcome, the fact that teachers may or may not be readily available becomes an important factor in deciding on a mode of training. Vocational teachers are normally required to have about five years of practical experience at the trade before they are permitted to train others. In addition they may be required to take a six-month course in pedagogy before being authorized to teach. The availability of vocational instructors thus depends to some degree on the number of craftsmen available for training. One of the most common ways to train vocational teachers is to upgrade the skilled craftsman by giving him a series of courses in pedagogy. In addition to such upgrading, however, the individual must also be offered a compensation that motivates him to shift careers and spend time taking courses in education. In some societies the prestige of a teacher is so great that little effort is needed to motivate skilled workers to shift careers. Where such prestige exists and vocational training researchers are readily available, then training in the schools has a distinct advantage. In some situations teachers of regular academic subjects shift to vocational teaching by learning a specific craft. It is also possible for an individual to go through a regular teacher-training program with a specialty in vocational teaching.

A successful training program needs competent administration. In some developing countries, however, the shortage of administrators is a critical factor in the whole process of industrialization. If there is such a shortage those with administrative skill and experience are likely to work in the sector offering the highest compensation. Government competition for administrators is likely to be strong. If compensation is the most significant factor, then administrators are more likely to work in industry where salaries are generally much higher than in a school system or a training institution. Only if the prestige of being affiliated with a training facility or program is very high will it offset the monetary lure of industry.

Summary

The choice of a mode of training will depend not on any pat answers but on the careful assessment of all relevant influences. Although economic factors are of course extremely important, they constitute only some of the elements that must be taken into account, and in actuality institutional and political factors sometimes determine the choice. Only with an overview of both economic and noneconomic considerations can the decisionmaker arrive at a judicious selection.

4

Evaluation of Vocational School Programs

The cost effectiveness of a mode of training varies with the type of program in which it is offered. Because the formal vocational school is the most popular type, the choice of training mode for an occupation or group of occupations will usually involve an analysis of school programs. This chapter therefore discusses various aspects of the programs commonly offered in vocational schools.

Program Characteristics

Included in the discussion of program characteristics are the duration of the training, specificity of courses and distribution of instruction time, cost of equipment, and compatibility of training with the production process in industry. The tables (1–23) present data on these characteristics.

Program duration. The length of a training program depends on the depth and breadth of the skills to be developed. In some programs broad training may be desirable to provide students with entry-level skills for several families of jobs within a general occupation or career cluster. In other programs depth may be preferable to develop skills within a single job family.

Consider, for instance, the electricity cluster which contains five basic job families: installation and maintenance, industrial electricity, electrical production, electromechanics production, and electromechanics service. Separate training programs may be geared to prepare students for entry into each of the families, or a single broad program may develop the general entry-level skills required by all families. The time needed to train a student for entry into a single family will be determined by the requirements of that program alone. But the duration of a program training students for the general field of electrical work—with appropriate skills for entry into all its families—is not necessarily calculated by adding up the requirements for the individual programs. Many elements of each program are common to all. In planning it is necessary to determine the duration of the program for each job family and also that of a program for the whole cluster of related families.

In addition it is important to determine the duration of the training program for each job in the hierarchy within each family. These data are needed to determine the most desirable location for advanced as well as entry-level training. If it takes 500 hours to train a general electrician, it may be advantageous to offer the first 250 hours in the vocational school and the second 250 hours in an industrial setting.

Besides its direct effect on the total cost of the program, the amount of time needed to complete the training will sometimes determine where it takes place. Much depends on the production or training cycle of the training institution. Programs in glazing and painting, for example, are relatively short, highly specialized, and may take only a few weeks or months. But a school must utilize its facilities much longer than this, and such short-term programs would not be economically justified without the likelihood of a continuous flow of students. At the other extreme, it takes much longer to train a carpenter than to construct a house. Unless a trainee can move to a new construction project and continue learning, his total training program may be adversely affected.

Specificity of courses and distribution of instruction time. The greater the percentage of instruction time, theoretical and practical, that can be shared by other programs, the greater the opportunity for economies of scale, and the more attractive the school setting for training. Since machinists must be able to read and interpret blueprints, most machinists' programs offer a course in drafting and blueprint reading. But electricians and carpenters also need these same skills. A shop for blueprint reading can therefore achieve economies of scale by training machinists, electricians, and carpenters together. Similarly, in order to advance in the machine trades a worker must know enough mathematics to adjust a machine or convert from fractions to decimal measurements. Classroom instruction in basic mathematics is a necessary part of many programs, and economies of scale can be achieved easily in institutions that offer a variety of programs requiring mathematics. In contrast, training for auto body repair requires very little time in other shops, and the program is not closely related to any other instruction. In this case a training institution that offers a variety of programs has no special advantage of economies of scale.

Cost of equipment. For certain programs it is obvious that the cost of equipment will be so high that it can be justified only on the basis of high utilization. A computer would be relatively expensive to acquire just to train programmers. But the school may offer many courses in computer programming and operations and use the machine for other instructional or administrative purposes. If the computer use is thus increased the cost per student or per hour of instruction may be reduced enough so that the acquisition of a computer by the school would be an attractive alternative to offering the program in a plant.

The total cost and hours of use determine the feasibility of acquiring equipment. Specialized equipment—say, in a machine shop—that does not relate to other programs can only be justified by the number of students who use it. A lathe may be used only a few hours a day to train machinists, but if its rate of obsolescence is low and its lifetime sufficiently long it may still serve enough students to be worth purchasing for a vocational school. A numerically controlled machine, however, is economically justified even in industry only by very high utilization and would require almost continuous use in a school to make its cost per student attractive.

Compatibility of training with the type of industry. The possibility of shifting programs from school to plant depends partly on whether the industry's normal production process is conducive to training for the occupation

Table 1. Auto Body Instruction Time

Item	General	Specific
Hours of instruction		
Class		
General academic	0	0
Related theory	40	0
Laboratory		
Arc welding	90	100–200[a]
Auto body	500	100–300[a]
Sheet metal	40	0
Total	670	200–500
Percentage distribution of instruction time		
Class		
General academic	0	0
Related theory	6	0
Laboratory		
Shared	19	0
Specific	75	100

a. Program duration depends on the specialty such as painting, body or glass work, or frame straightening.

in question. General programs may be offered in many industries. Electricians and pipe fitters, for example, do the same type of job in many different industries and can be trained almost anywhere. Other programs are more specific to the industry and can be trained only in that industry: a textile worker can be trained only in a textile factory. The availability of training facilities outside the school is limited by the size of the particular industry.

The higher the job in the hierarchy, the more limited the opportunity for training in industry. A mechanic may learn his skills in a great many industries; engine mechanics in a smaller number; and turbine-engine mechanics in still fewer industries.

Some occupational skills cannot be developed in the job environment where the trainee will eventually work but must be mastered in another industry that offers the particular training required. Construction workers assembling structural steel need to know welding and riveting, but a construction site is not the best place to train welders; instead they can learn to weld in the welding industry. The size of the industry's labor force and the proportion of the occupation in the labor force also affect the possibility of on-the-job training.

Distribution of Instruction Time—Raw Data

Tables 1 through 11 summarize the distribution of instructional hours for each of the occupational clusters and job families considered in this study. On the basis of these data it is possible to determine what facilities and equipment will be required for a proposed enrollment mix. The data can also be used in analyzing instructional programs, the transferability of skill, and allocation of costs.

Each table refers to a cluster of occupations which require a significant amount of the same theoretical and practical instruction. Each cluster is divided into separate families of jobs which share learning experiences. These families are then further subdivided into two or three levels of skill or instructional requirements, ranging from the minimum skills required for entry into the job group to advanced specialization within that group. The following definitions have been used:

Entry: The student has acquired the basic practical skills required for the craft. He is thoroughly capable of performing safely under direction but does not have sufficient knowledge to work independently and determine what actions should be performed. This classification corresponds approximately to designations X-YY.10 of the International Labour Organisation (ILO).

Advanced: The student possesses all the basic manipulative skills and associated theoretical knowledge necessary to plan and perform the

Table 2. Construction and Woodworking Instruction Time

Item	Carpentry			Cabinetmaking	
	Entry	Advanced	Specialized	Entry	Advanced
Hours of instruction					
Class					
General academic	0	30	90	0	0
Related theory	100	190	110	90	240
Laboratory					
Drafting	0	20	20	0	50
Woodworking	50	100	0	320	400
Construction	150	650	200–400[a]	0	0
Cabinetmaking	0	0	0	290	410
Total	300	990	420–620	700	1100
Percentage distribution of instruction time					
Class					
General academic	0	3	15–21	0	0
Related theory	33	20	18–26	13	22
Laboratory					
Shared	17	12	5–10	0	5
Specific	50	65	47–58	87	73

Transferability of instruction (percent)	Carpentry	Cabinetmaking
Theory		
Carpentry	—	50
Cabinetmaking	20	—
Practical		
Carpentry	—	50
Cabinetmaking	10	—

a. Specialist programs range from those for roofing or framing (up to 200 hours) to concrete framing (up to 400 hours).

general tasks of his craft. This classification corresponds approximately to ILO designations X-YY.20 to X-YY.50.

Specialized: The student possesses all the skills of an advanced craftsman plus the additional theoretical and/or practical knowledge to operate specialized machinery or perform other functions of a highly specialized nature that require advanced competency. This classification corresponds approximately to ILO designations X-YY.60 and above.

The tables show the distribution of instruction time in each program in both hours and percentages. All hours represent approximations of the amount of time spent in the class or laboratory identified in the left-hand column. Classroom hours are divided between general and related instruction. General academic courses—primarily math and science—are appropriate to many programs and, more specifically, may be taught by one teacher. The tables are based on the assumption that no general instruction is offered in courses such as language or history. Related theory refers to classroom instruction specifically appropriate to the occupational program. It can be assumed that this is taught by the same instructor who conducts the laboratory associated with the program; these hours should therefore be added to the laboratory hours when allocating staff costs.

Data on the distribution of laboratory hours provide information as to which programs share specific facilities. The data can be used as a basis for planning programs and allocating costs of shared laboratories. In the development of these tables it has been assumed that each program has access to a laboratory specific to its own needs. When this is not the case, facilities required for instruction must be provided in the main laboratory. For instance, if a school intends to offer a program in sheet metal but not welding, the sheet-metal laboratory must provide enough welding stations to offer the 70 hours of welding instruction identified in Table 10.

Classroom and laboratory hours are then shown as percentages of the total program time. Class time is again divided between general academic instruction and related theory. The data for laboratory hours are combined to show what percentage of total instruction time is spent in laboratories shared by other programs and what percentage is spent in the laboratory planned specifically for the program under consideration. For instance, in

Table 3. Drafting Instruction Time

Item	General	Specific
Hours of instruction		
Class		
General academic	0	0
Related theory	50	50
Laboratory	690	400–820[a]
Total	740	450–870
Percentage distribution of instruction time		
Class		
General academic	0	0
Related theory	7	6–11[a]
Laboratory		
Shared	0	0
Specific	93	89–94

a. Variability in both related theory and laboratory work depends on the area of specialization.

Table 4. Electricity and Electromechanics Instruction Time

Item	Installation and maintenance		Industrial electricity and electronics			Electro-mechanics
	Entry	Advanced	Entry	Advanced	Specialized[a]	
Hours of instruction						
Class						
General academic	0	50	0	0	70	0
Related theory						
Electricity	70	120	70	100	140	100
Electromechanics	0	0	70	120	180	100
Electronics	0	50	30	50	400	0
Laboratory						
Drafting	0	30	40	40	40	70
Basic electricity	300	450	300	375	450	250
Electromechanics	0	75	100	150	200	300
Electronics	0	50	80	110	110	0
Total	370	815	690	935	1590	820
Percentage distribution of instruction time						
Class						
General academic	0	8	0	0	4	0
Related theory	19	14	24	29	50	26
Laboratory						
Shared	0	24	6	4	2	38
Specific	81	55	70	67	44	36

Transferability of instruction (percent)	Installation and maintenance	Industrial electricity and electronics	Electro-mechanics
Theory			
Installation and maintenance	—	50	50
Industrial electricity and electronics	50	—	50
Electromechanics	50	50	—
Practical			
Installation and maintenance	—	70	50
Industrial electricity and electronics	70	—	50
Electromechanics	50	50	—

a. In such fields as radio and television, radar, or communications systems.

the piping and plumbing program described in Table 9 drafting and welding are assumed to be offered in laboratories shared by other programs, while piping is assumed to be taught in a laboratory planned specifically for this purpose. Thus at the entry level 21 percent of the laboratory instruction time is spent in shared laboratories and 53 percent in the lab specific to the program. This tabulation of percentages indicates the possibility of offering training in a noninstitutional setting. Programs in which a high percentage of time is allocated to general academic and/or shared laboratory instruction would be considered better possibilities for an institutional setting than would programs in which a high percentage of time is spent in related theory and/or a single unshared laboratory.

In most instances the three levels of skill in each family constitute a hierarchy in a single job ladder. That is, advanced skills build directly on basic or entry skills, and specialized skills develop directly from advanced skills. Progress in the hierarchy of instruction is therefore essentially linear, and all hours identified for advanced job skills include the hours required for the development of basic skills. As Table 2 shows, an advanced cabinet-maker requires 410 hours of instruction in cabinetmaking while a cabinet-maker at the entry level requires only 290 hours. This means that the advanced student receives 120 hours of instruction in addition to those in the basic course.

There are, however, some instances in which progress is not linear, and specialization does not incorporate the same instruction as that for advanced skills. This is especially true in mechanics and machine shop where advanced study is usually interpreted to mean broader generalization while specialization may ignore much of what the advanced general student studies and apply a proportionally greater time to specialized tasks. For instance, Table 8 shows that an advanced, general machine shop student receives 600 to 800 hours of instruction in the machine shop, while a single machine specialist receives only about 400 hours. The specialist may receive 300 or more of his hours on a single type of machine, however, while the generalist receives only about 100 hours on each of six machine types.

In the case of pure linear hierarchies of jobs within the same family, it can be assumed that 100 percent of the instruction given to a trainee at a lower level can be applied toward training for a higher position. Because not all hierarchies are linear, however, there is not always a high degree of interchangeability of students being trained for different levels of specialization within the same job family. In a given occupation cluster all families might share a great deal of instruction at the entry level, but there might be little similarity among their requirements for advanced positions. When planning programs which respond to a nation's broad needs for manpower it is desirable to know both how much of a training program can be transferred to other levels of specialization within the same family and how much can be transferred to another family within the same cluster.

Table 5. Electronics Instruction Time

Item	Installation		Maintenance			Industrial		
	Entry	Advanced	Entry	Advanced	Specialized	Entry	Advanced	Specialized
Hours of instruction								
Class								
General academic	80	80	80	100	240	80	100	100
Related theory								
Electricity	70	70	70	0	0	70	0	0
Electronics	0	150	200	300	400	300	350	400
Laboratory								
Electronics	190	500	500	630	700	500	630	770
Drafting	40	40	40	40	40	40	40	40
Total	380	840	890	1070	1380	990	1120	1310
Percentage distribution of instruction time								
Class								
General academic	19	7	10	9	17	9	9	8
Related theory	19	20	30	29	29	37	31	0
Laboratory								
Shared	12	5	5	4	3	4	4	3
Specific	50	68	55	58	51	51	56	89

Transferability of instruction (percent)	Installation	Maintenance	Industrial
Theory			
Installation	—	75	50
Maintenance	20	—	40
Industrial	30	25	—
Practical			
Installation	—	65	40
Maintenance	25	—	25
Industrial	35	40	—

Table 6. Engine Mechanics Instruction Time

Item	Entry	Advanced	Specialized
Hours of instruction			
Class			
General academic	0	50	0
Related theory	50	300	0
Laboratory			
Welding	0	50	0
Auto mechanics	200–500	600–900	100–300
Total	250–550	1000–1300	100–300
Percentage distribution of instruction time			
Class			
General academic	0	4–5	0
Related theory	10–20	23–30	0
Laboratory			
Shared	0	2–3	0
Specific	80–90	62–70	100

For programs such as welding, sheet metal, piping and plumbing, engine mechanics, drafting, and auto body which have no family subdivisions it is meaningless to consider the degree of transferability of instruction to other levels and job families. Because these programs are characterized by only one core program there is no question of sharing large units of instruction with other families. Furthermore, most of these programs offer a hierarchy of multiple specializations, only the more advanced of which have been considered in developing these tables. It would therefore be difficult to generalize about the degree of transferability which exists between the core program and the instruction required for each of the many specializations. These data can be derived only on the basis of specific programs.

In other clusters—like construction and woodworking, electricity, electronics, and heating and refrigeration, all of which contain several distinct families of related jobs—it is appropriate to consider interfamily transferability of instruction for purposes of program planning and evaluation. For these clusters Tables 1 through 11 present data on program transferability. They show the percentage of both theoretical and practical instruction in each family which may be applied toward the development of skills required in other jobs in the cluster. For instance, Table 5 shows that in electronics 75 percent of the theoretical instruction and 65 percent of the practical instruction for the average student in the installation program can be transferred to training maintenance personnel, while only 50 percent of the theoretical and 40 percent of the practical instruction can be transferred to a program in industrial electronics. In developing these tables, no attempt

Table 7. Heating, Refrigeration, and Air Conditioning Instruction Time

Item	Heating-plant maintenance		Refrigeration		General heating and refrigeration	
	Home	Industry	Home	Industry	Home	Industry
Hours of instruction						
Class						
General academic	50	50	100	100	100	100
Related theory	70	120	200	200	250	300
Laboratory						
Drafting	40	40	40	40	40	40
Welding	0	40	0	40	0	40
Sheet metal	70	70	70	70	70	70
Electricity and electromechanics	50	100	50	100	50	100
General mechanics	50	50–100	50	50	50	50
Plumbing and piping	25	50	25	50	25	50
Refrigeration	0	0	200	300 }	300	400
Heating	200	300	0	0	300	1150
Total	555	820–870	735	950	885	1150
Percentage distribution of instruction time						
Class						
General academic	9	7	14	11	11	11
Related theory	13	14–15	27	23	28	26
Laboratory						
Shared	42	48	33	36	27	28
Specific	36	30	26	30	34	35

Transferability of instruction (percent)	Heating-plant maintenance	Refrigeration	General heating and refrigeration
Theory			
Heating-plant maintenance	—	50	100
Refrigeration	50	—	100
General heating and refrigeration	80	90	—
Practical			
Heating-plant maintenance	—	33	100
Refrigeration	33	—	100
General heating and refrigeration	66	66	—

has been made to correlate specific curricula at each level of skill among all the families of the same cluster. Rather, these numbers are based on some indefinite "average" mix of students within each family. Therefore the transferability percentages are not directly related to the distribution of hours presented in the tables, but should be regarded simply as best available estimates of the overall characteristics of an average program.

The data presented in Tables 1 through 11 represent a synthesis of course syllabi from instructional programs offered in many parts of the world. Specific sources for these data include the curricula from community colleges and technical institutes in the United States, technical schools throughout Europe, selected European apprenticeship programs, and company-sponsored training programs from many parts of the world. These data on the distribution of course hours should not, however, be considered as a model for purposes of curriculum development. Actual curricula should be based on the requirements of the specific programs to be taught. The actual hours assigned to any one course will also depend on the organization of the individual institution. For instance, in a school operated on a quarter system a 75-hour course may be shortened to 5 hours a week for 13 weeks (total 65 hours), while in a school with a semester plan the same course may be drawn out to 5 hours a week for 18 weeks (total 90 hours).

Table 8. Machine Shop Instruction Time

Item	Machine tool operation (general)	Single machine specialty [a]	
		Entry	Advanced
Hours of instruction			
Class			
General academic	30	0	0
Related theory	90	30	50
Laboratory			
Drafting	70	0	0
Welding	50	0	0
Machine shop	600–800	100	400
Inspection and testing	100	0	50
Total	940–1140	130	550
Percentage distribution of instruction time			
Class			
General academic	3	0	0
Related theory	8–10	23	10
Laboratory			
Shared	27–37	0	17
Specific	52–60	77	73

a. For example, lathe, milling machine, or screw machine operation.

Table 9. Piping and Plumbing Instruction Time

Item	Entry	Advanced	Specialized [a]
Hours of instruction			
Class			
General academic	0	150	150
Related theory	50	200	300
Laboratory			
Drafting	0	150	50–200
Welding	40	100	100
Piping	100	250	300
Total	190	850	900–1050
Percentage distribution of instruction time			
Class			
General academic	0	18	15
Related theory	26	24	30
Laboratory			
Shared	21	29	25
Specific	53	29	30

a. For example, gas and steam fitting or sprinkler fitting.

In these tables it is assumed that the hour distributions are essentially independent of geographical location. Given students of similar quality and educational background, it should take the same amount of time to train an auto engine mechanic in Nigeria as in Peru, Singapore, or the United States. This assumption is based on the facts that the same basic occupational requirements will be imposed on a mechanic anywhere he works, that programs in developing countries are usually copied from those of developed countries, and that there is little association between culture and skills. There are, however, exceptions based on differences in pedagogy and objectives. Most western countries have developed their programs around broad general training, while developing countries have often attempted to train specialists at relatively low levels in the hierarchies of each job family. While this practice is now generally considered to be inefficient in the light of long-range plans for developing the economy and human resources, it is still common. Where such lower level specialization is of significance, as in the case of roofers and form-builders in the construction industry, special comments are made in the appropriate tables.

Interpretation of the Tables

The following example is offered as a guide for interpreting the data in Tables 1 through 11 and is based on an analysis of the construction and woodworking program in Table 2.

Hours of instruction by type of class and laboratory. The total hours of instruction for each level in each job family include both the class and laboratory hours. Thus a program to train entry-level carpenters would require approximately 300 hours:

> 100 hours of related theory
> 50 hours of woodworking
> <u>150</u> hours of construction
>
> 300 total hours

To develop the more comprehensive skills required of an advanced carpenter would require 990 hours of instruction:

> 30 hours of general academic instruction
> 190 hours of related theory
> 20 hours of drafting
> 100 hours of woodworking
> <u>650</u> hours of construction
>
> 990 total hours

It should be noted that the 190 hours of instruction in related theory required of an advanced carpentry program represents the *total* hours of instruction in this area and is not *in addition* to that required at the entry level. In other words, advanced carpentry requires 90 hours of instruction in related theory over and above the entry-level program.

Table 10. Sheet Metal Instruction Time

Item	Entry	Advanced	Specialized
Hours of instruction			
Class			
General academic	240	240	100
Related theory	50	320	250
Laboratory			
Drafting	70	70	40–70
Welding	70	70	70
Sheet metal	640	760	250
Total	1070	1460.	710–740
Percentage distribution of instruction time			
Class			
General academic	22	16	13
Related theory	5	22	35
Laboratory			
Shared	13	10	17
Specific	60	52	35

Table 11. Welding Instruction Time

Item	Gas welding	Arc welding	Combination
Hours of instruction			
Class			
General academic	40	40	40
Related theory	70	70	70
Laboratory			
Drafting	70	70	70
Gas welding	350	0	350
Arc welding	0	350	350
Total	530	530	880
Percentage distribution of instruction time			
Class			
General academic	8	8	5
Related theory	13	13	8
Laboratory			
Shared	13	13	8
Specific	66	66	79
Transferability of instruction (percent)			
Theory			
Gas welding	—	75	100
Arc welding	75	—	100
Combination	100	100	—
Practical			
Gas welding	—	10	100
Arc welding	10	—	100
Combination	100	100	—

Specialist programs represent a slightly different problem because the training programs required to develop these skills are generally not linear extensions of a basic or entry program. Table 2 shows that a carpentry specialist such as a roofer requires approximately 110 hours of related theory, but this should not be interpreted to mean that a specialist requires only 10 hours of instruction beyond that at the entry level. The theory learned by the entry trainee is related to many areas of construction while the specialist receives instruction in only one area. Thus the specialist may share as little as 20–40[1] hours of instruction with the entry trainee and take 60–80 hours of instruction to which the entry trainee would not be exposed.

1. This is an approximation made for discussion purposes only. Specific data relative to the degree to which programs within a family can share common courses were not computed during this study and would have to be derived on the basis of individual programs and curricula.

In all tables the data for each family should be treated independently of the data for other families in the same table. While there may be some courses in common these commonalities are shown only under transferability of instruction and cannot be derived from the data on hours. For instance, the 240 hours of related theory required by an advanced cabinetmaker represent a 150-hour increase over the instruction required at the entry level (240 − 90 hours), but it is totally unrelated to the 100, 190, and 110 hours of instruction in related theory required by entry, advanced, and specialist carpenters.

Distribution of instruction time. Under the subhead "Distribution of instruction time" the data on instructional hours are presented as percentages of the total. Thus Table 2 reports that an entry carpenter receives 100 hours of instruction in related theory out of a total 300-hour program. This data is reported under distribution of instruction time as 33 percent of the training program. The percentages for both general academic and related theory are derived directly from the class hours listed above under the comparable headings, divided by the total hours of instruction.

The percentages for laboratory time, shared and specific, however, represent slight modifications of the data listed above for laboratory hours. Here the subhead "Specific" indicates the percentage of instruction which would normally be offered in a laboratory designed specifically for the family under consideration; while the subhead "Shared" designates the percentage of instruction offered in laboratories which would normally be provided for other programs. For instance, 65 percent (650 ÷ 990) of the instruction in advanced carpentry takes place in the carpentry laboratory, while 12 percent (100 hours in woodworking plus 20 hours in drafting divided by 990 total hours) takes place in laboratories which are primarily for other programs.

Transferability of instruction. The data reported under this subhead identify the percentage of the total curriculum of a given family that is common to other families in the same cluster. Thus in Table 2, 50 percent of the theory—which refers to both general academic and related theory instruction—offered to students in an average carpentry program also applies to cabinetmaking. Similarly, approximately 20 percent of the theory offered to students in the average cabinetry program is common to the curriculum requirements of the average carpentry program.

The numbers reported in the transferability of instruction sections of the tables are highly subjective and cannot be rigorously substantiated. For example, in the derivation of the data reported in Table 2, it was assumed that an average program in carpentry would train most students in only entry-level skills because there are a great many opportunities to develop advanced carpentry skills in industrial settings. The average student in a cabinetry program, however, is assumed to receive advanced training. Therefore 50 percent of the 100 hours of theory instruction required for an average carpentry program is approximately the same as 20 percent of the 240 hours of theoretical instruction required for an average cabinetmaker. Similarly, 50 percent of the 200 hours of practical instruction (50 hours in woodworking and 150 hours in construction) required of the average carpentry student is approximately the same as 10 percent of the 860 hours of practical instruction (400 hours of woodworking, 410 hours of cabinetmaking, and 50 hours of drafting) received by an average cabinetmaker.

Cost and Utilization of Equipment

Tables 12 through 22 summarize the cost of equipment for the laboratories required by each of the programs considered in this study. The matrices also indicate the importance of the equipment to the programs for which it is used. The relationship between the equipment and the instructional program is shown by the number of hours which a student in each family uses each piece of equipment. The range of hour requirements corresponds to the range of career programs from entry to specialized as shown in Tables 1 through 11.

Table 12. Auto Body Laboratory: Cost and Utilization of Equipment

Equipment	Cost (U.S. dollars, 1972)	Priority	Program hours
Program specific			
Spray booth	4000–6000	2	—
Spray painting equipment	600–1000	1	25–100
Frame straightener *or*	8000–10,000 ⎫	1	50–150
Damage dozer	1,000–3000 ⎭		
General			
Hoist (lift)	2000–5000	1	General support for all programs.
Sheet metal brake	6000–8000	1	
Slip roll former	200–300	1	
General support			
Basic Equipment[a]	7000–10,000	1	—
Benches	150	g[b]	—
Miscellaneous tools	50–80 a student	g	—

g: General support equipment for the program as a whole.
Note: A priority rating of 1 indicates that the equipment is absolutely essential to the program; 2, desirable but not essential; 3, a luxury.
a. Including jacks, grinders, sanders, drills, buffers.
b. Usually provided in a ratio of one for every five students.

Table 13. Construction and Woodworking Laboratory: Cost and Utilization of Equipment

Equipment	Cost (U.S. dollars, 1972)	Carpentry		Cabinetmaking	
		Priority	Program hours	Priority	Program hours
Program specific[a]					
Lathe	600	3		1	
Bowl lathe	800	3		2	
Jointer (6″)	300	1		1	
Jointer (12″)	1700	2		1	
Planer (8″ x 24″)	3000	2		1	
Router	260–650	3		1	
Panel saw	400	1	General support equipment.	2–3	General support for all carpentry and cabinetmaking programs.
Belt and disc sander	400	2		1	
Radial arm saw (16″)	1550–1710	1		1	
Tilting arbor saw	450–1050	2		2	
Bend saw	1500–2000	2		1	
Scroll saw	300	2		1	
Shaper	500–600	2		1	
Bench saw	350–600	1		1	
Drill (15″)	75–320	1		1–2	
Trimmer (veneer)	15	x		1–2	
Mortiser	950	x		1–2	General support for advanced instruction.
Tennoner	1000	x		1	
Spray booth	950	x		1	
Spray gun	30	x		2	
Dip tank	—	x			
General support					
Benches	200 a student	g	—	g	— —
Miscellaneous tools	50–70 a student	g	—	g	— —
Basic equipment[b]	2000–3000	g	—	g	—

g: General support equipment for the program as a whole.
x: Equipment unrelated to the needs of the particular job family.
Note: A priority rating of 1 indicates that the equipment is absolutely essential to the program; 2, desirable but not essential; 3, a luxury.
a. One of each item required regardless of class size.
b. Including power drills and saws, grinders, buffers, and hand routers.

Table 14. Drafting Laboratory: Cost and Utilization of Equipment

Equipment	Cost (U.S. dollars, 1972)	Priority	Program hours
Program specific			
Drafting tables			
Large	460	1–2	400–600
Small	140	1	200–400
Drafting machine[a]	150	1–2	—
Tracing tables	470	2	0–50
General support			
Blueprint machine	600	1–2	—
Blueprint	150	1–2	—
Tools and supplies	75 a student	g	—

g: General support equipment for the program as a whole.

Note: A priority rating of 1 indicates that the equipment is absolutely essential to the program; 2, desirable but not essential; 3, a luxury.

a. One for each large table.

In addition to the hours of utilization, the relationship between machines and skill families is noted with a priority rating from 1 to 3. A rating of 1 indicates that the equipment is absolutely essential to the program to which it is related; a priority of 2 indicates equipment which is desirable but not essential; while a priority of 3 indicates equipment that is somewhat of a luxury. The number of hours a piece of equipment is in use by a student in a specific program is not always linked to its priority. Some equipment, such as a saw in a woodworking program, may be used only a small portion of the time, but it is essential to have such a power saw if the student is to be able to prepare lumber for further work. Often a different priority is assigned a single piece of equipment in several different programs. For instance, a mortiser is an essential piece of equipment in a furniture-making program, but it is merely very desirable in a cabinetry program, and has no use at all in general carpentry.

Table 15. Electricity and Electromechanics Laboratory: Cost and Utilization of Equipment

Equipment	Cost (U.S. dollars, 1972)	Installation and maintenance		Electricity and electronics		Electromechanics	
		Priority	Program hours	Priority	Program hours	Priority	Program hours
Program specific							
Industrial electricity lab	13800	2	50–100	1	150–200	2	50–100
Basic electricity bench (wired)	100 a station	1		1		1	
Wiring test panels	300	1					
Motor starter panel	4000–6000	3	Time requirements depend on specific program objectives.	2	Time requirements depend on specific program objectives.	1	Time requirements depend on specific program objectives.
AC switchboard	1800	3		2		1	
DC switchboard	1500	3		2		1	
Slip ring DC	250	3		2		1	
Squirrel-cage induction	250	3		2		1	
3-5 HP synchronous	4000	3		2		1	
Exciter switchboard	2000	2		2		2	
High-tension transformer	130	2		1		2	
Motor trainer systems	4000–5000 for 15 stations	2	50–100	1	50–100	1	100–200
Power supply	4000	g		g		g	
General support							
Tools	75–100 a student	g		g		g	
Basic electricity kit	250 a student	1	50–100	1	50–100	1	50–100
Materials[a]	100 a student	g		g		g	

g: General support equipment for the program as a whole.
Note: A priority rating of 1 indicates that the equipment is absolutely essential to the program; 2, desirable but not essential; 3, a luxury.
a. Including light fixtures, service boxes, and meters.

Tables 12-22 are intended to provide a basis for computing total laboratory costs. The cost data were derived from the catalogs of different manufacturers and represent an approximate average of the list prices, which varied according to the type, quality, and country of origin of the equipment. Although costs are expressed in 1972 dollars and are therefore out of date, the figures provide an idea of the relative cost of different types of equipment. These relative prices do not change considerably over time and can be used to compare the program costs of alternate curricula. Hours of use are another approximation derived from existing vocational programs in several countries. The tables thus offer basic data for planning and developing curricula for different modes of training and provide another measure of the feasibility of noninstitutional training.

Table 16. Electronics Laboratory: Cost and Utilization of Equipment

Equipment	Cost (U.S. dollars, 1972)	Priority	Program hours
Program specific			
Television trainers	500–800 each	1 ⎫	Time requirements
Communications trainer	3500–4000	1 ⎬	depend on specific
Digital logic trainer	400–1200	1 ⎭	program objectives.
General			
Complete electronics test console	3000	g	
Electronics benches (instrumented)	400–500 a station	g	
General support			
Electronics benches (general)	100 a station	g	
Basic equipment[a]	250 a station	g	
Tools	75 a student	g	
Supplies[b]	600 a station	g	

g: General support equipment for the program as a whole.
Note: A priority rating of 1 indicates that the equipment is absolutely essential to the program; 2, desirable but not essential; 3, a luxury.
a. Including power supplies and test equipment.
b. Including electronics training kits at $200 a student and instruction boards.

Table 17. Engine Mechanics Laboratory: Cost and Utilization of Equipment

Equipment	Cost (U.S. dollars, 1972)	Priority	Program hours	
			General	Specialized
Program specific				
Valve resurfacer	1000	1–2	10–20	50–150 for brake mechanic.
Brake service equipment	2500–3000	1–2	10–20	60–100 for tune-up mechanic.
Electronic engine analyzer	1000–2000	1–2	40–80	
Engine dynamometer	5000–7000	2	40–80	
Chassis dynamometer	7000–10,000	2–3	30–60	50–100 for front-end mechanic.
Front end alignment	2000–3000	1		100–200 for tune-up mechanic.
Engines				
Gasoline	500–1500 new	1	150–300	
Diesel	2000–3000 new	2–3	50–100	
Diesel fuel injection system	1000–3000	2–3	20–50	150–250 for transmission mechanic.
Transmissions				
Standard	250+	1 }	40–80	
Automatic	250+	1		
Chassis	1000	1	40–75	50–100 for front-end mechanic.
Generator test bench[a]	500–1000	2	30–50	
General				
Engine degreaser	1000	2–3 }		
Welding equipment (gas)	200–400	1		General support for all programs.
Wheel balancer	100–200	1		
Hoists (lifts)	2000–5000	1		
General support				
Basic equipment[b]	12,000–15,000	1	—	—
Miscellaneous tools	75–100 a student	g	—	—
Benches	150	g[c]	—	—
Instructional kits[d]	50–150 each	2–3	—	—

g: General support equipment for the program as a whole.
Note: A priority rating of 1 indicates that the equipment is absolutely essential to the program; 2, desirable but not essential; 3, a luxury.
a. Including armature lathe and other related repair equipment.
b. Including jacks, lubrication equipment, engine stands, parts cleaner, tire changer, miscellaneous grinders, presses, compressor, spark plug cleaner.
c. Usually provided in a ratio of one for every three students.
d. Electrical system trainer, fuel system trainer, and the like.

Table 18. Heating, Refrigeration, and Air Conditioning Laboratory: Cost and Utilization of Equipment

Equipment	Cost (U.S. dollars, 1972)	Refrigeration and air conditioning				Heating			
		Home		Industry		Home		Industry	
		Priority	Program hours	Priority	Program hours	Priority	Program hours	Priority	Program hours
Program specific									
Refrigeration cycle trainer									
Industrial	3000–4000	1	1–200	1	150–250	x		x	
Home	1800	x		1	100–150	x		x	
Compressor and refrigeration system									
Water cooled	500	1	50–100	1	50–100	x		x	
Air cooled	500	1	50–100	1	50–100	x		x	
Air-conditioning trainer	1000	1	25–50	x		x		x	
Heat pump	2000	3	Optional	x		x		x	
Gas oil burner trainers	400–700	x		x		1	50–100	1	50–100
Burner test equipment	1000	x		x		1		1	
Heating trainer (home)	2000[a]	x		x		1	100–200	1	100–200
Boiler (industry)	—[b]	x		x		3		1	75–100
General support									
Benches	100	g		g		g		g	
Tools and supplies	80–100 a student	g		g		g		g	

g: General support equipment for the program as a whole.
x: Equipment unrelated to the needs of the particular job family.
Note: A priority rating of 1 indicates that the equipment is absolutely essential to the program; 2, desirable but not essential; 3, a luxury.
a. At least two systems, one each for forced air and hot water with interchangeable gas and oil burners, are usually required.
b. The size of a boiler usually prohibits the installation of one for instruction only. The heating system for the facility itself is usually used for teaching purposes.

Table 19. Machine Shop Laboratory: Cost and Utilization of Equipment

Equipment	Cost (U.S. dollars, 1972)	Number of stations[a]	General		Single machine specialty	
			Priority	Program hours	Priority	Program hours
Program specific			Priority and hours depend on the special characteristics of each program.		Priority and hours depend on the specific objectives of the program.	
Lathe (12"), bare	660					
Accessories	250	8				
Lathe (15"), precision	5000					
Lathe (11"), turret	3100					
Lathe (13"), turret	6900					
Milling machine (horizontal)	4200–7000					
Accessories	1000	4				
Milling machine (vertical)	1200–2700					
Shaper	600–1200					
Punch press	3500	1				
Screw machine	160–230	1				
Boring machine	5000	1				
Surface grinder	5000	1				
Cylinder grinder	1200	1				
Grinder, tool cutter (6")	255	1				
Radial gear lead drill	7000	1				
Electronic discharge machine	10,000–12,000		3	0–100		
Tape punch	2000		3	40–80		
Controller	48,000		g			
Tracking unit (3 axis)	2500		g			
General support						
Basic equipment[b]	4000–5000		g			
Ancillary tools and equipment	75 a student		g			
Benches	170 a station		g			

g: General support equipment for the program as a whole.
Note: A priority rating of 1 indicates that the equipment is absolutely essential to the program; 2, desirable but not essential; 3, a luxury.
a. In a 20-station general shop.
b. Including miscellaneous drills, grinders, air compressors, and the like.

Table 20. Plumbing and Piping Laboratory: Cost and Utilization of Equipment

Equipment	Cost (U.S. dollars, 1972)	Priority	Program hours
General support[a]			
Benches	200	g	—
Basic equipment[b]	2500	g	—
Tools	75 a station	g	—
Supplies	50 a station	g	—

g: General support equipment for the program as a whole.

a. Except for benches, which are required for each student, all equipment in this laboratory is used as general support for all programs in piping and plumbing.

b. Including power hacksaw, pipe threader, pipe bender, welding system.

Distribution of Workers within Industries

Table 23 was derived from the occupational structures of industries in a group of developing countries.[2] When used with data collected on the site as to plant size (number of employees), this table provides a guideline for determining the feasibility of training on the job. Training for a given occupation is more readily offered on the job or through a combination program the larger the plant and the higher the proportion of workers with that occupation in the labor force. For example, if a country has a large machinery industry in-plant programs for machine shop occupations can be contemplated because, as shown in Table 23, 15 to 20 percent of the total employed in that industry are machine shop operators. But the machine shop industry would be no place to train piping and plumbing occupations because they constitute less than half of one percent of the labor force in that industry.

2. Given in Morris Horowitz, Manuel Zymelman, and Irwin Herrnstadt, *Manpower Requirements for Planning: An International Comparison Approach*, Vol. 2 (Boston, Mass.: Northeastern University, 1966).

Table 21. Sheet Metal Laboratory: Cost and Utilization of Equipment

Equipment	Cost (U.S. dollars, 1972)	Priority	Program hours
Program specific			
Bender	400	1	
Brake (box and pan)	1200	1	
Brakes folder	700	1	
Folder	340–850	1	
Seaming machine	475	1	General support for all
Notching and shearing machine (6" x 6")	400	1	programs. Approximately
Grooving machine	500	1	50 percent of all shop
Roll former, manual	250	1	time is spent on ma-
Power	550	2	chines, uniformly distrib-
Slip roll former	200–300	2	uted among all types.
Punch and shear	400	1	
Shear	250–400	1	
Shear (ring and circle)	1600	1	
Shear (rotary)	570	1	
Shear (cutoff), manual	1000	1	
Power	2000–5000	1	
Shear (squaring)	1300	1[a]	
Welder, AC only	325	2[a]	General support; not a
AC/DC	425	2	work station.
Spot	280	1[a]	
Torch, portable	350[a]	1	
Burring machine	50		
General support			
Benches	200	g	—
Basic tools	60–80 a student	g	—

g: General support equipment for the program as a whole.
Note: A priority rating of 1 indicates that the equipment is absolutely essential to the program; 2, desirable but not essential; 3, a luxury.
a. Basic instruction in welding provided in the welding laboratory.

Table 22. Welding Laboratory: Cost and Utilization of Equipment

Equipment	Cost (U.S. dollars, 1972)	Priority	Program hours		
			Arc	Gas	Combination
Program specific					
Oxyacetylene welding	250[a]	1	x	250–300	250–300
Arc welding (booth and welding)	1000	1	160–200	x	160–200
Welder	850–1500	1	20–50	x	20–50
Wire	800	2	0–40	x	0–40
Spot	200	1–2	0–20	x	0–20
Heliarc	1500	2	20–40	x	20–40
Portable spot	525	3	0–10	x	0–10
Soldering bench	200	2	0–10	20–50	20–50
General					
Brake (box and plan)	700	2[b]	General support for all programs, 50–100 hours.		
Slip roll former	160	2[b]			
Hardness tester	350	1[c]			
Tensile tester	450	1[c]			
Weld tester	200	1[c]			
General support					
Basic equipment	3000[d]	g			
Miscellaneous tools	50–75 a student	g			
Benches	150 a station	g[e]			

g: General support equipment for the program as a whole.
x: Equipment unrelated to the needs of the particular job family.
Note: A priority rating of 1 indicates that the equipment is absolutely essential to the program; 2, desirable but not essential; 3, a luxury.
a. Including bench, vent hood, and basic torch system and accessories.
b. May be shared with sheet metal laboratory.
c. Should be included in comprehensive materials testing facility associated with machine shop.
d. Including basic oxyacetylene manifold system, power hacksaw, pipe bender, drill, grinder.
e. Usually provided in a ratio of one for every five students as general support.

Table 23. Occupational Distribution of Workers within Industries per Thousand Employees

Industry	Carpentry	Drafting	Electricity	Engine mechanics	Machine shop	Piping and plumbing	Sheet metal	Welding
Chemical	3–5	3–6	9–12	1–3	12–20	7–10	1–2	7–10
Construction	175–225	2–4	30–40	2–4	3–5	45–60	6–10	2–4
Electrical machinery	4–6	16–20	80–120	0–1	60–80	1–2	6–10	12–17
Furniture	25–30	5–7	0–1	0	1–3	0–1	1–2	1–2
Machinery	4–8	25–30	8–11	2–3	150–200	3–4	8–12	18–30
Metal products (fabricated)	3–5	10–12	7–10	5–7	50–80	5–10	10–15	25–30
Paper	3–4	3–4	10–15	0–1	8–15	3–6	1–2	3–5
Petroleum	6–10	5–7	10–15	3–4	5–8	23–30	1–2	10–12
Railroads	5–8	1–2	4–6	0–1	3–4	3–4	2–4	5–8
Textiles (mill products)	3–4	0–1	4–5	0	4–7	1–2	0–1	1–2
Transportation (motor vehicles)	20–30	5–8	12–20	175–200	70–100	3–6	20–30	40–50
Utilities	5–8	10–14	85–115	6–10	5–12	30–50	1–2	5–8

Note: Separate categorizations are not available for auto body, cabinetry, electronics, and heating and refrigeration.

5

Evaluation of a Proposal
for Vocational Training

This chapter provides a way to evaluate proposals for vocational training. A final decision to choose one mode of training over another should of course take account of all factors, including institutional and political ones, but the procedure outlined here is a systematic way of reaching a logical economic choice.

The methodology is portrayed in the flow chart on pages 84-5. It is assumed that initially a proposal for a vocational school is submitted for consideration, but it need not be that of a vocational school. The procedures that follow could be applied to the evaluation of any mode of vocational training such as a skill center, a rapid retraining system, or an in-plant program. The chart is designed in such a way that irrespective of the type of proposal the evaluator will be in a position to compare it with other modes of vocational training. The arrows in the chart show the direction of the steps in the sequence. The numbers in the blocks are keyed to explanations of the chart that are given in the text.

1. *Proposal for a vocational school offering training*
   for y trainees in program x

The proposal for a vocational school should ideally provide the following information:
   a. Type of programs to be offered in the school
   b. Number of students expected in each program every year for at least five to seven years, or for the lifetime of the equipment

    c. Number and types of laboratories
    d. Number and types of machines in each laboratory
    e. Cost of each laboratory
    f. Areas of classrooms, laboratories, and other facilities
    g. Costs per unit of area
    h. Cost of land
    i. Number of instructors
    j. Salaries of instructors
    k. Annual cost of administration, including maintenance
    l. Annual cost of materials and supplies
    m. Other costs
    n. Hours of classroom and laboratory instruction for each program
    o. Time required for graduation (in years)
    p. Length of school year
    q. Entry requirements for trainees

2. *Determine the probability of employment for graduates*

    a. Recent census data may provide unemployment rates by occupation, from which employment opportunities may be estimated.
    b. Special surveys may also indicate unemployment rates by occupation and can be used to calculate the probability of employment for graduates of training programs.
    c. Follow-up studies of graduates and dropouts from training programs would provide direct information on the probability of employment for graduates.
    d. Interviews with personnel managers of major firms and with union officials will turn up additional information on the employment of graduates of training programs.

3. *Compare job entry requirements with qualifications conferred by program*

Job requirements vary from country to country. Nevertheless, basic information can be obtained from the International Standard Classification of Occupations of the International Labour Organisation; the *Dictionary of Occupational Titles,* U.S. Department of Labor; and from interviews with experts in industry and the ministry of labor in the country concerned. In addition many large firms, especially multinationals, are likely to have detailed descriptions of each job in the plant, with requirements for each. Qualifications conferred by training can be obtained from instructors and directors of the training institutions. Interviews with graduates from training programs as well as supervisors on the job can provide information on any discrepancy between entry requirements and the ability actually acquired in the training program.

In certain industries union membership is a prerequisite for a job. This is based on the theory that union membership assures a certain level of competence. Actually, however, the practice may be no more than an indication of the monopolistic authority of the union. Other prerequisites for hiring may include a primary or secondary school diploma or a certificate indicating completion of an apprenticeship program or vocational school. Some firms are prepared to hire untrained persons with a certain minimum level of schooling if they agree to enter the firm's training program.

4. *Determine employers' preferences in hiring*

A small firm that is in no position to have its own training program nevertheless must hire new workers every so often to replace those who died, quit, retired, or were fired. If the manager has a free choice what kind of worker does he employ? He may prefer a person who was trained in a public vocational school. Or he may prefer someone who completed a program in an industry-sponsored training center. In most cases his choice is probably based upon limited personal experience or upon the reputation of the training programs. It is unlikely that a small employer has had actual experience with all the different varieties of training programs and made a rational choice based upon his concern about effectiveness. Nevertheless he indicates his preference by hiring a worker from one training program instead of another.

Larger firms have a wider choice. Through their hiring practices they can support the type of training they prefer, or they can set up their own program. The latter choice may be a vote of no confidence in the various outside training programs. But sometimes firms prefer to train workers to fit their own narrow needs and thus reduce turnover because a narrowly trained worker is generally less mobile.

The attitude of industry toward training can be obtained by interviewing company managers, especially personnel directors. Questions such as the following have to be asked:

a. Why are trainees from one program hired in preference to trainees from other programs?

b. Has the company had experience with employees from other programs?

c. Have the trainees from the preferred program actually performed better on the job as craftsmen? Are their wages higher?

d. Have trainees from the preferred program been advanced more rapidly to supervisory positions?

A sample survey of company officials of large and small firms from a range of industries could elicit sufficient detailed information on the above questions to guide in the selection of the mode of training. Current employees are commonly used by companies to recruit new workers, especially at the blue-collar level. Obtaining information on this practice is not easy because it is done informally. Interviewing a sample of employment managers of large firms will give some indication of how widespread the practice is. Interviewing a small sample of newly hired workers will also provide a clue for hiring preferences.

Other avenues by which employers recruit workers include private employment agencies and newspaper and other advertisements. In nations where private employment agencies are permitted, they are more commonly used for white-collar and professional workers. Interviews with such agencies are also recommended.

5. *Determine cost per graduate in each program*[1]

Total costs of a program are:

$$TC_j = PC_j + EC_j + MC_j + FC_j$$

where TC_j = total costs of program j
PC_j = personnel costs of program j
EC_j = equipment costs of program j
MC_j = cost of materials for program j
FC_j = cost of facilities for program j.

Personnel costs. There are generally two types of personnel: administrative and instructional. The latter are in turn divided into laboratory and classroom instructors. Since the costs of a program are estimated on the basis of existing programs, only average costs are considered.

$$PC_j = ADM_j + LP_j + ClP_j$$

where ADM_j = cost of administrators allocated to program j
LP_j = cost of laboratory personnel allocated to program j
ClP_j = cost of classroom personnel allocated to program j

1. A numerical example is given in Appendix A.

Costs are allocated on the basis of student hours of instruction for a given program as compared with total student hours for all programs in the school.

$$ADM_j = TCA \times \frac{HRS_j}{\sum\limits_{j=1}^{n} HRS_j}$$

where TCA = total cost of administrators
   HRS_j = student hours in program j.

$$LP_j = \sum\limits_{k=1}^{m} TCLI_k \times \frac{HRSL_{kj}}{\sum\limits_{j=1}^{n} HRSL_{kj}}$$

where $TCLI_k$ = total cost of instruction for laboratory of type k
   $HRSL_j$ = student hours of laboratory instruction in program j
   m = number of laboratories of type k.

$$CII_j = TCCII \times \frac{HRSCI_j}{\sum\limits_{j=1}^{n} HRSCI_j}$$

where $TCCII$ = total cost of classroom instruction
   $HRSCI_j$ = student hours of class instruction in program j.

Equipment costs. The cost of equipment is figured by using the following formula:

$$EC_j = \sum\limits_{k=1}^{m} TLC_k \times \frac{H_{kj} \times S_j/SS_{ij}}{\sum\limits_{j=1}^{n} H_{kj} \times S_j/SS_{ij}}$$

where TLC_k = total cost of equipment for laboratory k
   H_{kj} = total number of instructional hours spent in laboratory k by students in program j
   S_j = number of students in program j. This is the number of students that will be trained on the equipment over its lifetime, not the number of students in program j in a given year
   SS_{ij} = student stations per unit of equipment i

$$m = \frac{\sum\limits_{j=1} H_{kj} S_j}{\text{class size} \times \text{duration of class (in hours)}},$$

and $\quad TLC_k = \sum\limits_{i=1}^{v_i} EC_{ik} + FC_k$

where EC_{ik} = equipment cost of item i used in laboratory k

FC_k = fixed costs of laboratory k (equipment needed to support machines on which students learn),

and $\quad EC_{ik} = r_i \times C_i$

where v_i = number of machines of type i

C_i = unit cost of machine i.

$$r_i = \frac{\sum\limits_{j=1}^{m} HRS_{ij} \times S_j/SS_{ij}}{HRSA_i \times u_i}$$

where HRS_{ij} = hours of instruction on machine i required by a student in program j

$HRSA_i$ = hours available on machine i

u_i = utilization factor of machine i.

Cost of materials. The costs of materials and supplies are very difficult to estimate. Because they vary from one activity to another and in accordance with the intensity of the training they have to be determined case by case.

Cost of facilities. The total construction cost allocated to program j ($TCCP_j$) is:

$$TCCP_j = \sum\limits_{k=1}^{m} TLCC_k \times \frac{H_{kj} \times S_j}{\sum\limits_{j=1}^{n} H_{kj} S_j} + TCICC \times \frac{HRSCl_j}{\sum\limits_{j=1}^{n} HRSCl_j} (1 + BF)$$

where $TLCC_k$ = total construction cost of laboratory k

$TCICC$ = total classroom construction cost

BF = building factor (allowance to cover overhead space, hallways, offices, washrooms, and the like) which ranges between .4 and .6

$TLCC_k = AREA_k \times CPA_k$

$TCICC = AREA_{cl} \times CPA_{cl}$

$AREA_k$ = area of laboratory k

$AREA_{cl}$ = area of classrooms

CPA_k = construction cost per unit of laboratory k area

CPA_{cl} = construction cost per unit of classroom area.

6. *Determine capacity utilization of facilities, equipment, and personnel*

Capacity utilization is a relative concept: it is the actual use of capacity as a percentage of a normal measure of capacity. For example, normal capacity of a laboratory may be 30 hours a week multiplied by the number of students that can be taught effectively at one time in the laboratory. Normal instructor capacity might be 15 students multiplied by five hours daily. Given the type of laboratories and programs in the school, the hours of laboratory and class instruction, and the number of students in each program it is possible to calculate utilization of capacity. For example:

$$\frac{\text{Utilization}}{\text{of laboratory capacity}} = \frac{\sum\limits_{k=1}^{m} \sum\limits_{j=1}^{n} HRS_{kj}}{\sum\limits_{k=1}^{m} HRS_{nk}}$$

where HRS_{kj} = hours in laboratory k spent by students in program j
HRS_{nk} = normal capacity in student hours of laboratory k.

Capacity utilization of teachers can be approximated by the student-teacher ratios of classrooms and laboratories separately. In general, utilization of less than 70 percent of normal capacity should encourage a revision of the program or of the number of students in it.

7. *Determine the rate of return for program* x

The rate of return is usually calculated on the basis of occupational earnings by age adjusted by the probability of employment. These data are not readily available in many developing nations. Moreover the soundness of using present earnings of older people to represent future earnings of today's entrant to the labor market is highly questionable. It is therefore advisable to confine the computations to earnings for the first five years from occupations obtainable after training and those that workers would have held without training. It can be assumed that the difference between the earnings of the two types of occupations remain constant thereafter. The rate of return can be calculated with the following equation:

$$I_t = \frac{E_{t1} - E_{w1}}{(1+r)} + \frac{E_{t2} - E_{w2}}{(1+r)^2} + \ldots + \frac{E_{t5} - E_{w5}}{(1+r)^5} + \ldots + \frac{E_{tn} - W_{wn}}{(1+r)^n}$$

where I_t = investment in vocational training
E_{t1} = earnings of an individual with training in year 1
E_{w1} = earnings of an individual without training in year 1.

Data on earnings can be obtained from interviews in a few typical plants, employment bureaus, or labor unions.

8. *Compare cost per graduate of vocational and academic schools*

In many developed and developing countries graduates from the academic stream compete successfully for jobs with graduates from vocational schools. In this case if the type of student input is similar for both schools a comparison of the cost per graduate may provide a clue to the economic viability of vocational education. In general it should be expected that education in vocational schools is more expensive than in regular academic schools. When the discrepancy is more than 30 percent, however, a closer scrutiny of the vocational programs must be made.

9. *Survey training modes in existence in the country*

Vocational training may be offered in a wide variety of institutions.

Public schools. Information on government-sponsored training in the public school system is generally readily available. A description of the training can usually be obtained from the ministry of education or in some situations from the ministry of labor and would include information on a whole range of items such as programs, facilities, teachers, students, and administration. To fill in all the details it may be necessary to visit a small sample of schools.

Private schools. In some countries training programs are offered to the public by private schools for profit. Information on them can frequently be obtained from the ministry of education, which in most countries requires the registration of private schools. If a list of such schools is available, a sample could be visited to obtain data similar to that listed above. If such a list is not available, some sample names may be obtained from telephone books and by talking to a few large firms who might hire graduates of private schools.

Training in the enterprise. There is always the likelihood that employers, especially the large ones, have developed some type of training in their plants, but there is not apt to be a list of such firms, and it will be necessary to search out this information. A brief list of large firms can be put together quickly from conversations with knowledgeable persons in the government or in industry associations.

Training centers. Vocational training may also be offered in a specially designed center administered by a government agency, an employer association, or some industry federation. In most situations the center offers training in a limited number of semiskilled or skilled occupations, with special emphasis on the practical or shop aspects of the work. When appropriate to the job, theoretical, mathematical, and blueprint-reading courses are also offered. If training centers are run by government agencies there is no problem in locating the facilities. If run by private organizations, the centers can be found by addressing the various employer associations or industry federations that administer them. If a facility with good programs is available it may be relatively easy to expand training there, especially if its location and equipment fit the needs of the growth industries.

Apprenticeship programs. Apprenticeship programs are likely to be found in many countries and may be sponsored by an employer or an industry group, possibly in cooperation with a government agency or union. Programs sponsored by an industry group, a government agency, or a union are readily located; those sponsored by individual employers, especially small ones, will not be easy to find. By interviewing a few key leaders in the major industries and unions, however, the location and general characteristics of most apprenticeship programs can be learned. A number of individual employers should also be interviewed to get some feel of their reactions to apprenticeship.

In addition to general and descriptive information about the operation of apprenticeship programs, it also is necessary to get answers to the following:

a. What are the government laws affecting apprenticeship (minimum age, minimum wage, ratio of apprentices to journeymen, benefits to firms employing apprentices)?

b. How are apprenticeship programs financed?

c. How much related instruction is required of apprentices?

d. Who provides the facilities, administers the courses, and finances the related instruction?

e. Do the apprentices attend the related instruction on their own or company time? Is it mandatory?

f. What are the requirements for entering an apprenticeship program?

g. What is the length of the program?

h. What is the pay scale for apprentices?

i. How are the apprentices recruited?

j. What is the retention rate?

k. Do the graduates receive a special certificate that is recognized nationwide?

l. Is the apprenticeship system operating at capacity? If not, how many additional apprentices can it absorb?

Much of this information will be obtained through interviews with key individuals in industry, unions, and government, either general officers of organizations or specialized personnel responsible for the administration of apprenticeship programs. While it may vary among industries or occupations, apprenticeship does offer a mode of training that normally can be expanded rather easily, within certain limits.

Other training modes. It is rather common for a foreign firm to bring skilled personnel into the country to train nationals. Depending on how long the firm has been operating there it might be a significant source of newly trained workers. Such foreign firms are easily identified and located, and an interview would elicit the desired information about any training program. In some nations the military offers training courses to new recruits which often cut across civilian occupations. Again, one or two interviews could easily uncover information on such programs.

It is not likely that one can collect all the material on the various training systems and programs of a country in a short time. Locating sources of information will undoubtedly be a problem, and even when they are located interviews can consume valuable time and hold up the process of evaluation. In order to minimize delays, key persons should be interviewed at the initial stage of any investigation. The following is a checklist of organizations and officials who should be approached for information about training programs:

    a. Ministry of education
    b. Ministry of labor
    c. Military leaders
    d. Trade union leaders
    e. Officials of industry federations
    f. Officials of employer associations
    g. Officers of major firms
    h. Training directors of school programs
    i. Training directors of skill centers
    j. Training directors of company-run programs

10. *Calculate present cost per graduate of this mode*

The cost of any mode of training in an institutional setting is calculated like that of a regular vocational school. In the case of training offered partly in a noninstitutional setting (apprenticeship or on-the-job training) the noninstitutional segment has to be calculated separately. When different programs share the same resources in the noninstitutional setting the allocation of costs can be made on the basis of hours of instruction or hourly use of equipment. The major part of the cost of training in noninstitutional settings is the opportunity cost of skilled workers and supervisors engaged in teaching, opportunity cost of machinery and equipment, and cost of breakdown of equipment. There are no statistics available to allow an analysis of these costs. Data will have to be developed on the site, and even then the best observations will be only gross approximations of reality.

11. *Determine the mode's capacity to absorb y extra trainees*

The present cost per trainee or graduate gives no indication of the cost of absorbing an increased number of trainees, especially if the program uses idle equipment and personnel from other systems or institutions. In many countries, for example, rapid retraining programs use the facilities of vocational schools and the equipment of factories at night or during other nonworking hours and consequently show a low cost per trainee. Once the available free capacity is totally taken up, however, the marginal cost of training increases considerably. The same can be said about on-the-job training. As long as the number of trainees or apprentices is small it is possible to take advantage of the excess teaching capacity of skilled workers and supervisors. When the number increases substantially, it may be necessary to hire extra personnel with the result that training costs may differ considerably from the costs before the enlargement of the program.

12. *Determine if training of y extra trainees would be profitable to the firm*

$$\sum_{t=1}^{m} \frac{C_t + W_{at} - Q_{at}}{(1+r)^t} < \sum_{t=m+1}^{n} \frac{Q_{st} - W_{st}}{(1+r)^t}$$

where C_t = cost of training
   W_{at} = apprentice wages during training
   Q_{at} = value of apprentice production
   Q_{st} = value of production of a skilled worker
   W_{st} = wages of a skilled worker
   t = time subscript
   r = rate of discount

Costs of training can be calculated as above (10).

13. *Consider different policies to make training attractive to the firm*

Ways to encourage training in the enterprise are to:
   a. Provide the administrative machinery for cooperative training efforts by small enterprises to lower the cost per trainee
   b. Subsidize training through grants for each trainee
   c. Subsidize trainees' wages
   d. Make funds available at preferential interest rates for the construction of training facilities and the purchase of machinery and equipment
   e. Provide support personnel and materials to lower the cost of training to the enterprise

14. *Calculate explicit and implicit costs of policies*

Explicit costs of the policies are easily calculated. A flat grant per trainee multiplied by the number of trainees gives the total cost of subsidizing training; the cost of the administrative setup for overseeing training as well as the subsidy of lower interest rates can also be calculated. The implicit costs of policies are more difficult to determine: a strong in-plant training program at the expense of formal vocational schools may alienate the formal bureaucracy of a ministry of education or labor. If this policy is financed by taxation of a particular sector of the economy there might be adverse political reactions. A sounding of local industrial and political leaders is the only way of gauging the impact of these policies.

15. *Explore the possibilities for developing new modes of training*

If it is decided that the existing modes of training in the country are inadequate, a search must be made for new ones. There are numerous possibilities based on different combinations of on- and off-the-job training. The following lists the kind of information needed to evaluate new modes of training in a school or training center and in a plant.

A. Schools and training centers
1. Facilities
   a. Possible location of each facility
   b. Size of each facility
   c. Maximum number of trainees that can be handled in a facility
2. Programs
   a. Availability of curricula
   b. Sources of materials for programs and courses
   c. On what basis will they be selected
3. Administration
   a. Who will select the courses and programs to be offered
   b. Size and organization of the administration
   c. Job placement activities
4. Students
   a. Qualifications and standards for admission
   b. How will the students be recruited
   c. Qualifications for graduation
5. Teachers
   a. Training and experience required
   b. How will teachers receive their training and what is the duration of that training
   c. How will vocational instructors be recruited
   d. How will instructors' wages compare with those of craftsmen in industry

6. Output factors
    a. Expected rates of dropping out and completion
    b. Estimated cost of a graduate
    c. Reputation of graduates
    d. Employability of graduates

B. In-plant training
    1. Facilities
        a. Possible location of the training by industry
        b. Number and location of plants
        c. Training capacity per occupation
    2. Programs
        a. Courses and programs available
        b. Description of possible methods of training
        c. Duration of training program
    3. Administration
        a. Who will select the courses and programs to be offered
        b. Who will select the trainees and on what basis
        c. Who will supervise training
    4. Trainees
        a. What are the requirements to enter program
        b. What incentives will be used to induce workers to enter training program
    5. Instructors
        a. Who will be the instructors
        b. What special training will be given to them
        c. What will be the ratio of instructors to trainees
        d. Will instructors also have production or supervisory responsibility in the plant
    6. Output factors
        a. Estimated cost of a graduate
        b. Retention rate of trainees
        c. Reputation of trainees

The list is by no means all-inclusive, and there are numerous combinations of school and enterprise training. Other major questions for which answers must be sought are:

What are the attitudes of the participants toward a new mode of training? How are those concerned with the existing modes of training expected to react toward competition from the new mode?

What measures are necessary to overcome possible opposition on the one hand, and encourage the necessary cooperation on the other?

In the final analysis the possibility of establishing a new form of vocational training depends on a variety of circumstances that must be evaluated in toto. Only an approach that combines all the economic, educational, and institutional variables can provide a guideline for action.

Flow Chart A for Evaluating a Proposal for Vocational Training

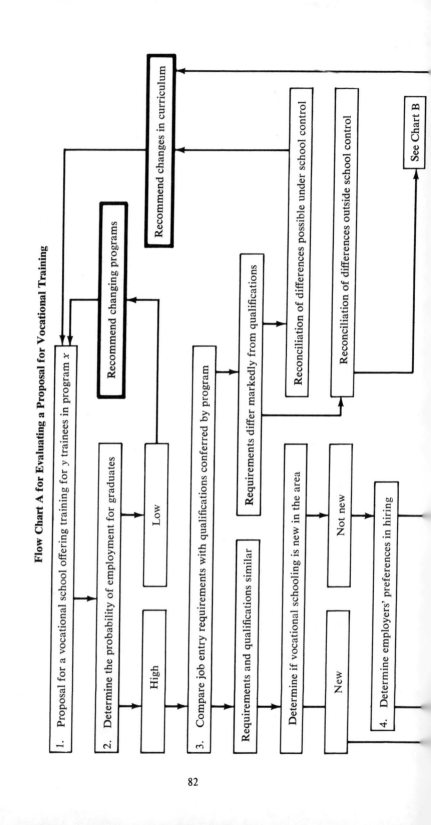

1. Proposal for a vocational school offering training for y trainees in program x

2. Determine the probability of employment for graduates

   High

   Low

3. Compare job entry requirements with qualifications conferred by program

   Requirements and qualifications similar

   Requirements differ markedly from qualifications

   Determine if vocational schooling is new in the area

   New

   Not new

4. Determine employers' preferences in hiring

Recommend changing programs

Recommend changes in curriculum

Reconciliation of differences possible under school control

Reconciliation of differences outside school control

See Chart B

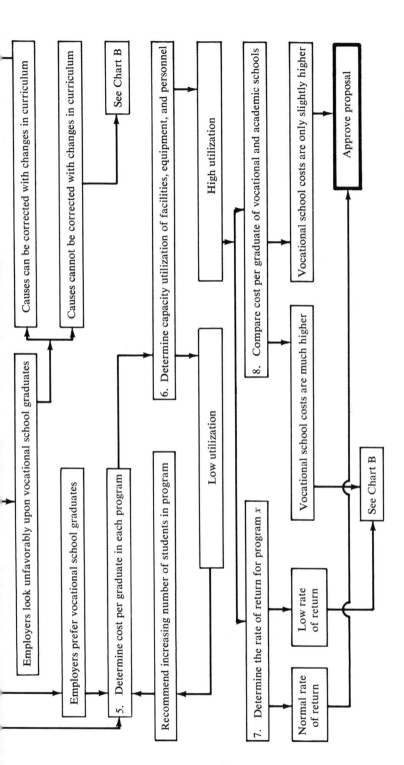

Causes can be corrected with changes in curriculum

Causes cannot be corrected with changes in curriculum

See Chart B

Employers look unfavorably upon vocational school graduates

Employers prefer vocational school graduates

6. Determine capacity utilization of facilities, equipment, and personnel

High utilization

5. Determine cost per graduate in each program

Recommend increasing number of students in program

Low utilization

8. Compare cost per graduate of vocational and academic schools

Vocational school costs are only slightly higher

Approve proposal

Vocational school costs are much higher

7. Determine the rate of return for program x

Low rate of return

See Chart B

Normal rate of return

Flow Chart B for Evaluating a Proposal for Vocational Training

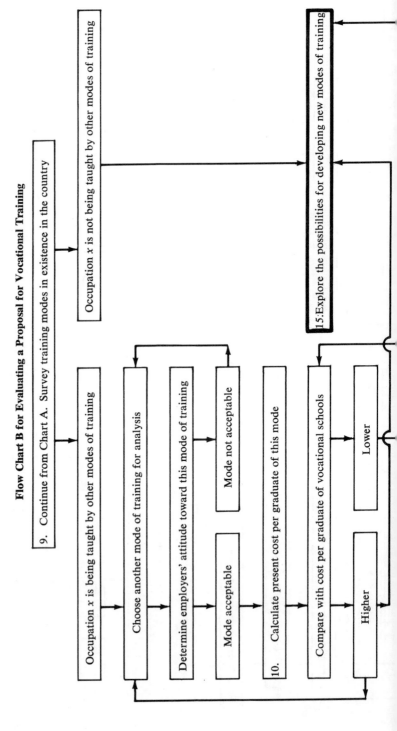

9. Continue from Chart A. Survey training modes in existence in the country

Occupation *x* is not being taught by other modes of training

Occupation *x* is being taught by other modes of training

Choose another mode of training for analysis

Determine employers' attitude toward this mode of training

Mode acceptable

Mode not acceptable

10. Calculate present cost per graduate of this mode

Compare with cost per graduate of vocational schools

Higher

Lower

15. Explore the possibilities for developing new modes of training

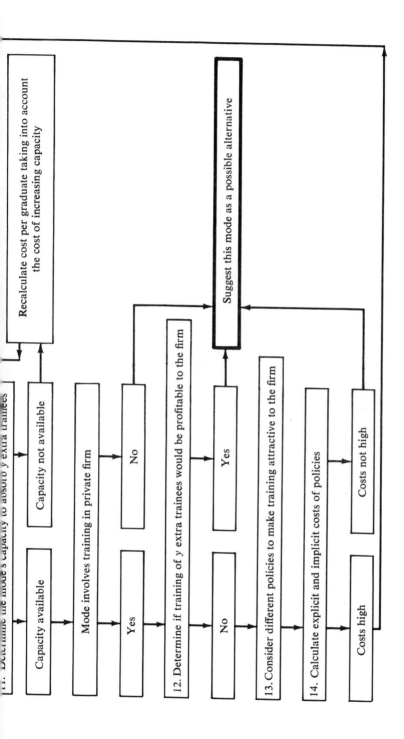

11. Determine the mode's capacity to absorb y extra trainees

Capacity available

Capacity not available

Recalculate cost per graduate taking into account the cost of increasing capacity

Mode involves training in private firm

Yes

No

12. Determine if training of y extra trainees would be profitable to the firm

Yes

No

Suggest this mode as a possible alternative

13. Consider different policies to make training attractive to the firm

14. Calculate explicit and implicit costs of policies

Costs high

Costs not high

85

Appendix A

A Numerical Example of the Calculation of the Costs of a Training Program

The following example computes the cost of training in a hypothetical welding program that is being offered in conjunction with other programs. This appendix is intended to demonstrate the use of the data in Tables 1 through 11. Since these sample calculations make several general assumptions about other programs offered in a hypothetical school, the results should not be used as a basis for evaluating welding programs in general.

Basic Assumptions

All operating costs, enrollment projections, instruction hours, and the like are based on single-year figures, and the entire welding instruction is assumed to take place in the course of a year. This assumption is also valid when the program is offered over a period of years if there is a steady inflow of students (steady state).

The average annual demand for the welding program is assumed to be:

    25 gas (oxyacetylene) welders

    10 arc welders

    15 combination welders

Enrollment in other programs that also use the welding laboratory is assumed to be:

    Sheet metal: 35 students a year

    Machine shop: 30 students a year

Facilities shared by welding students with other programs are assumed to have the following costs and hours of instruction.

Drafting laboratory:

Equipment = $10,700

Facility costs = $45,000

Hours of instruction, not including welding = 15,000

Instruction costs = $8,000 a year

Classrooms:

Facility costs = $125,000

Hours of instruction of other programs, not including welding (ΣHRS_j) = 450,000 (300,000 hours laboratory; 150,000 hours class)

Instruction costs = $105,000 a year

Total administrative costs (TCA) are assumed at $35,000 a year.

The following subscripts are used in this example:

d = drafting j = program index

t = total k = laboratory index

w = welding i = equipment index

s = sheet metal m = machine shop

Administrative Costs

Administrative costs to be allocated to the welding program are computed using the following equation:

$$ADM_w = TCA \times HRS_w / \Sigma HRSj \tag{1}$$

where ADM_w = administration costs allocated to welding program

TCA = total costs of administration

HRS_w = student hours of welding program

ΣHRS_j = student hours of all programs.

With TCA and HRS_j known, the first step in computing the allocated costs of administration is to determine HRS_w. From Table 11 the total hours of instruction needed for gas, arc, and combination welders are 530, 530, and 880 respectively. These hours are then multiplied by the number of students in each program (25 gas, 10 arc, and 15 combination welders) to compute the total hours of welding instruction.

$$HRS_w = (530 \times 25) + (530 \times 10) + (800 \times 15) = 30,550 \text{ hours}$$

Then, by substituting into equation (1), the administrative costs to be allocated to the welding program are computed as follows:

$$ADM_w = 35,000 \times \frac{30,550}{450,000 + 30,550} = \$2,250 \text{ a year (rounded)}.$$

Cost of Laboratory Instruction

Laboratory instruction costs to be allocated to the welding program are computed by using the following equation:

$$CLI_w = \Sigma CLI_{kw} \qquad (2)$$

where $CLI_{kw} = TCLI_k \times \dfrac{HRSL_{wk}}{\Sigma HRSL_k}$.

As shown in Table 11, welding students use both welding and drafting laboratories. It is therefore necessary to compute for both the welding and the drafting laboratories the cost of instruction allocated to the welding program (CLI_{ww} and CLI_{dw}). On the assumption that related theory is also taught in the welding laboratory and that the same teacher teaches both components of the welding program, the total hours of instruction in the welding laboratory for gas, arc, and combination welders are 420, 420, and 770 respectively. These hours are then multiplied by the number of students in each program to compute the total hours of welding laboratory instruction.

$$HRSL_{ww} = (420 \times 25) + (420 \times 10) + (770 \times 15) = 26,250 \text{ hours}$$

CLI_{kw} = cost of laboratory instruction k in welding program
TCL_k = total cost of laboratory instruction k
$HRSL_{wk}$ = student hours of welding program spent in laboratory k
$\Sigma HRSL_k$ = total student hours of all programs spent in laboratory k

Similarly, from tables 10 and 8, the total number of hours that the welding laboratory is used by sheet metal ($HRSL_{sw}$) and machine shop ($HRSL_{mw}$) students equals 3,950 hours [(35 × 70) + (30 × 50)]. Thus, the total utilization is 30,200 hours (3,950 + 26,250). If we assume one welding instructor at a cost of $8,500 per year, equation (2) may be solved as follows:

$$CLI_{ww} = \$8,500 \times \frac{26,250}{30,200} = \$7,400 \text{ (rounded)}.$$

A similar computation for the drafting laboratory results in the following allocation of drafting instruction costs:

$$CLI_{dw} = \$8,000 \times \frac{70 \times (25+10+15)}{1500 + [70 \times (25+10+15)]} = \$1,500 \text{ (rounded)}.$$

The sum of these figures gives a total laboratory cost allocated to the welding program of:

$$CLI_w = CLI_{dw} + CLI_{ww} = \$1{,}500 + \$7{,}400 = \$8{,}900.$$

Cost of Class Instruction

Class instruction costs to be allocated to the welding program are computed using the following equation:

$$CCII_w = TCCI \times \frac{HRSC_w}{\Sigma_j HRSC_j} \tag{3}$$

where $CCII_w$ = cost of class instruction in welding program
$TCCI$ = total cost of class instruction
$HRSC_w$ = student hours of welding program spent in classroom
$\Sigma_j HRSC_j$ = student hours of all programs spent in classroom.

From Table 11 the class hours associated with each welding program are 40. This number is then multiplied by the total number of students in each program to give $HRSC_w$ as:

$$HRSC_w = (40 \times 25) + (40 \times 10) + (40 \times 15) = 2{,}000 \text{ hours.}$$

Then the total cost of class instruction allocated to the welding program becomes:

$$CCII_w = \$105{,}000 \times \frac{2{,}000}{(2{,}000 + 150{,}000)} = \$1{,}400 \text{ (rounded)}.$$

Equipment Costs

Equipment costs allocated to the welding program are computed in the following manner:

$$TCL_w = \sum_k (EC_{wk} + FC_{wk}) \tag{4}$$

where TCL_w = total cost of the laboratory welding program
EC_{wk} = equipment costs of laboratory k allocated to welding program
FC_{wk} = fixed cost of laboratory k allocated to welding program.

Because the welding students use both welding and drafting laboratories, equipment costs of these laboratories must be allocated to the welding program. These allocated costs are computed below.

The fixed costs of the welding laboratory are derived from Table 22:

Basic equipment	$3,000
General	1,860
Benches	600
Miscellaneous tools	1,500
FC_w = Total	$6,960

The cost of benches and miscellaneous tools is based on an enrollment of 20 students, with benches provided in a ratio of 1:5.

The equipment costs of the welding laboratory are computed as follows:

$$EC_w = \sum_i v_i C_i \qquad (5)$$

where v_i = number of machines of type i
        C_i = cost of machine of type i

and $v_i = \dfrac{\sum_j HRS_{ij} \times S_j / SS_{ij}}{HRSA_i \times U_i}$

where HRS_{ij} = hours of instruction on machine i required by a student in program j
        S_j = number of students in program j
        SS_{ij} = student stations on equipment i in program j
        $HRSA_i$ = hours available on equipment i
        U_i = utilization factor.

In a sample calculation of $v \times C$ for an arc-welding system (from Table 22), arc welders HRS = 160 to 200 hours (assume 180). For machine shop and sheet metal students, assume the instructional hours in welding are prorated according to the mix represented by the average combination student. (This assumption will probably be valid for most laboratory equipment computations.) Thus for machine shop and sheet metal students the hours on arc-welding equipment are:

$$HRS_{ws} = 70 \times \frac{180}{590} = 21.36$$

$$HRS_{wm} = 50 \times \frac{180}{590} = 15.08$$

where 70 and 50 refer to the hours of welding instruction received by sheet metal and machine shop students respectively (Tables 10 and 8), and 180/590 is the factor used to assign the hours of instruction received by sheet metal and machine shop students in the welding laboratory to arc-welding equipment. (180 is the average number of hours only arc-welding equipment is used; 590 is the average number of hours of instruction of a combination welding program using all equipment. See Table 22.) If one student is assumed for each station (SS_{ij} = 1), v_i for arc-welding stations is calculated as follows:

$$
v = \frac{\overbrace{(180 \times 15)}^{\substack{\text{combination}\\\text{welders}}} + \overbrace{(180 \times 10)}^{\substack{\text{arc}\\\text{welders}}} + \overbrace{(35 \times 21.36)}^{\substack{\text{sheet}\\\text{metal}}} + \overbrace{(30 \times 15.08)}^{\substack{\text{machine}\\\text{shop}}}}{1560 \times 0.75} = \frac{5,697}{1,170} \cong 5.
$$

In other words, approximately 5 arc-welding machines would be needed. This assumes that the equipment is available 30 hours a week × 52 weeks a year (1,560 hours) and that the rate of machine utilization is 75 percent. Because the average cost of one arc-welding booth and welder is $1,000, the total equipment cost for arc-welding systems is:

$$EC = v \times C = 5 \times \$1,000 = \$5,000.$$

Applying similar computations to all other systems results in a total cost for all welding equipment of approximately $12,400. If the fixed and equipment costs for the welding laboratory are combined the total cost of the welding laboratory is:

$$TLC_w = \$12,400 + \$6,960 = \$19,400 \text{ (rounded)}.$$

The amount of this total cost borne by the welding program is then computed from the following equation:

$$EC_{jk} = \frac{TLC_k \times H_{kj}}{\sum\limits_{j} H_{kj}} \tag{6}$$

where EC_{jk} = equipment costs of laboratory k allocated to program j
TLC_k = total cost of laboratory k
H_{kj} = hours use of laboratory k by program j
$\sum_j H_{kj}$ = hours use of laboratory k by all programs

$$EC_{ww} = \$19,400$$

$$\times \frac{(25 \times 350) + (10 \times 350) + (15 \times 700)}{(30 \times 50) + (35 \times 70) + (25 \times 350) + (10 \times 350) + (15 \times 700)}$$

$$= \$16,300 \text{ (rounded)}.$$

To compute the total laboratory costs allocated to the welding program, the allocated costs of the drafting program must be added:

$$EC_{wd} = 10,700 \times \frac{[(25+10+15) \times 70]}{15,000 + [(25+15+10) \times 70]} = \$2,000 \text{ (rounded)}$$

where $(25+10+15) \times 70$ represents the total hours of drafting instruction received by students in each of the three welding courses. The equipment cost to be allocated to the welding program is then the sum of the allocations from both the drafting and welding programs:

$$EC_w = \$2,000 + \$16,300 = \$18,300.$$

Facility Costs

The total facility costs allocated to the welding program include:

$TLCC_d = \$45,000$
$TCICC = \$125,000$
$TLCC_w = \$60,000$ (assumed).

Using the cost allocation factors $\left[(HRS_{kj} \times S_j)/(\Sigma_j HRS_{kj} \times \Sigma_j S_j)\right]$ for the welding program computed in the above section, the total facility cost to be allocated to the welding program is:

$$TCCP = \left[\left(45,000 \times \frac{3,500}{18,500}\right) + \left(60,000 \times \frac{26,250}{30,200}\right)\right.$$

$$+ \left.\left(125,000 \times \frac{(40+70) \times (25+10+15)}{150,000 + (40+70) \times (25+10+15)}\right)\right] [1+0.4]$$

$$= \$91,000 \text{ (rounded)}.$$

This assumes that 40 percent of the construction cost of the facility is allocated to noninstructional use, such as hallways and service areas.

Annual Variable Costs per Student

To calculate the annual average operating cost per student of the welding program, the following formula is used:

$$OCPS_w = \frac{ADM_w + CCII_w + CLI_w + C_m}{NOS_w} \tag{7}$$

where $OCPS_w$ = total operating cost per student of welding program

ADM_w = administrative cost of welding program

CLI_w = cost of laboratory instruction of welding program

$CCII_w$ = cost of class instruction of welding program

C_m = cost of materials. An amount of $50 a year for each student is assumed

NOS_w = number of welding students a year

$$OCPS_w = \left(\frac{2{,}250 + 1{,}400 + 8{,}900}{50}\right) + 50 = \$300 \text{ (rounded).}$$

Annual Fixed Costs per Student

The annual average fixed cost per student of the welding program is calculated as follows:

$$AFCPS_w = \frac{TCCP_w - FRV + EC_w}{TNOS_w}$$

where $AFCPS_w$ = allocated fixed cost per student in welding

$TNOS_w$ = total number of students in the welding program over the life of the program. For this example, assume the program is planned for 7 years; therefore $TNOS_w = 7 \times NOS_w = 350$.

$TCCP_w$ = total construction cost for welding program

FRV = facility recovery value (salvage value) after the welding program is discontinued. For this example, assume that after building depreciation is accounted for this factor represents 65 percent of the initial facility cost. Therefore, $FRV = TCCC_w \times 0.65 = \$57{,}800$.

Then

$$AFCPS_w = \frac{89{,}000 - 57{,}800 + 18{,}000}{350} = \$150 \text{ (rounded).}$$

Total annual average cost per student in welding $(ACPT_w)$ then becomes:

$$ACPT_w = AFCPS_w + OCPS_w = 300 + 150 = \$450.$$

In summary, the average cost of $450 per student for the welding program is obtained by determining the total cost of administration, laboratory instruction, class instruction, and equipment of welding and other laboratories, and the total construction costs, and allocating them to the welding program. The allocation is made on the basis of the number of classroom and laboratory hours for the welding program compared with the instruction time and use of facilities of all other programs. For the sake of simplification straight-line depreciation is assumed, and the influence of interest charges is disregarded.

Appendix B

An Analytic Framework
for Reviewing Evaluations
of Vocational Training

The review of selected literature (Appendix C) uses a comparative analytical approach based on a broad framework that encompasses many different variables. This comprehensive framework was developed to point out the pitfalls of extending to other cases the conclusions of a given evaluation of vocational training. Before comparisons are drawn it is necessary first to check out thoroughly the methodology, the variables, and the transferability of the conclusions to other situations. By applying this framework to the literature discussed in Appendix C, the reader can decide how much or how little of the conclusions cited are applicable when judging the cost-effectiveness of a mode of training.

The Framework

Included in the analytical framework are the following variables: purpose of the study; coverage of the study; type of evaluation, whether of process or output; characteristics of the trainee; costs of training—to the individual and to the vocational school, the enterprise, or the institution sponsoring the program; methods for determining special types of costs; benefits (outputs) to the individual, to society, and to the enterprise; choice of unit for determining outputs and costs; criterion for cost-benefit or cost-effectiveness analyses.

Purpose of an evaluation study. Evaluation studies are made for three basic purposes: to provide suggestions for improving a training program, to indicate the success or failure of a program, and to compare one system with another or with some standard of excellence to provide a rational basis for choosing the best method.

Coverage of the study. This variable has special significance when the conclusions of the study form the basis for major decisions, such as whether to expand a program drastically or to introduce an altogether new system of vocational training. Economies and diseconomies of scale are important considerations when determining the cost and size of an enterprise or labor market and assessing the value of output. If a comparative study of formal vocational schooling and apprenticeship programs shows that the cost of vocational schooling and the chances of getting a job through apprenticeship programs are both high, this does not prove conclusively that it is more cost effective to provide all training in apprenticeship programs. The vocational school may have marginal costs lower than average costs, that is, it shows economies of scale; the apprenticeship programs may share diseconomies of scale with marginal costs higher than average costs. In this case expanding the vocational school program might lower costs, and increasing the apprenticeship programs might increase costs.

Furthermore the ease with which apprentices find employment depends on the ratio of apprentices to openings, and the training of more apprentices might therefore make it harder for everybody to get a good job.

A distinction must also be made between studies that cover the whole training system under evaluation, only a part of it, or just a single enterprise. Reliability and extrapolation of the results will be different in each case.

Process evaluation. This type of study evaluates the entire training process in a specific system or school, including the administration, curriculum, teachers, teaching aids and equipment, type of building, and so on. The purpose of a process evaluation is to improve the ongoing system. But the results of these studies can also be used profitably to discover the advantages and disadvantages of different types of training, identify the training most commonly provided in different institutions, list the requirements for equipment and personnel, and compare occupational requirements with the curriculum offered. Most existing studies deal with process evaluation.

Output evaluation. This type of study evaluates the outcome of the training process and includes what happens to the trainee at the end of the program. When the output is compared with the cost of the process, cost-benefit or cost-effectiveness studies result.

Cost-benefit analysis can be a priori or a posteriori. The former is to ascertain the feasibility of a program not in operation. In the public sector a priori cost-benefit analysis is mostly used to make decisions on future investments such as for water supply, resource development, and especially defense. A posteriori studies are used to evaluate the output of existing or past programs and employ two basic approaches: before-and-after studies where the control is the individual before he enters the training system and control-group studies which compare groups of trainees with similar groups of untrained individuals.

The literature on output evaluation is sparse, and cost-benefit and cost-effectiveness studies are comparatively recent. Most studies deal with developed nations, very few with developing countries (see the Bibliography). There are almost no a priori studies of vocational training that include evaluation of output.

Characteristics of the trainee. Vocational training may be viewed as a process that receives an input—an individual with certain characteristics—and produces an output—the benefits that accrue to an individual, society, or training institution as a result of the training process. It is important to specify the kind of input when evaluating two separate processes, say, formal vocational schools and training systems outside the school. If the entrants in one come from a better environment, have a higher level of natural abilities, and are better motivated, then it will cost less to achieve the same level of proficiency with these candidates than with students of lower intelligence and poor motivation.

In specifying the input the following attributes must be described: age, background, previous education and experience, intelligence, and motivation. Many of these characteristics are specified in the requirements for admission and can be determined by studying the selection procedure if direct measurements are unavailable. Characteristics of the students or criteria for eligibility into the program are especially important in the before-and-after studies where the subject is his own control.

Costs. Costs have to be assessed for both the individual and the institution or firm providing the training.

For the individual in a vocational school the costs include fees charged by the school, books and materials, travel expenses in connection with the training, and opportunity costs of time spent in school while training, minus scholarships, board and room when provided by the school free, and other monetary support for travel and books.

For the individual in an enterprise the cost is the difference between the value of his contribution to production (marginal revenue product) and the wages he receives plus other fringe benefits. If the trainee in the enterprise is not employed there, his costs are the same as those of an individual in a vocational school.

For a vocational school the costs include salaries of teachers, administration, maintenance, materials, buildings and equipment, board and room (when offered), and scholarships, minus fees, other charges, and revenue from the sale of school production.

For an enterprise providing training direct costs include wages and salaries of instructors and administrators entirely employed in the training program and the cost and maintenance of buildings and equipment used only for training. Indirect costs include opportunity costs of existing facilities and equipment used for both training and production, the imputed value (opportunity costs) of supervisory personnel not directly involved in training, loss of production due to errors or spoilage, and incidental expenses related to training programs (travel, extra insurance needed to cover apprentices or trainees on the premises, board and meals, wages, and fringe benefits), minus the increased value of production attributable to trainees.

Some Controversial Issues in the Analysis of Costs

These issues include costs of new processes as against the old, joint costs, and value of production by the trainee in an enterprise.

New versus old processes. The age of a training program is an important variable which determines the actual costs of setting up the program and the value of buildings and equipment. Developing a curricula, training instructors, and setting up an administrative structure take time and money. These costs of setting up are relatively unimportant when considering an older program because in all probability they have already been amortized, but they may loom large in the appraisal of a new program.

Equipment costs are readily evaluated for a new program because the market value and depreciation of the machinery are easy to determine. The book depreciated value usually does not reflect market prices of used machinery, and in countries with high rates of inflation even a correct value has to be adjusted by a price index for the type of equipment.

Joint costs. When the same expenditure produces two different products, as when the same class is given for both general education and vocational students or the same equipment used by different cohorts of students, it is important to decide on what basis to prorate costs. There is no fast rule for cost proration. When dealing only with the marginal costs of economic production, consideration of joint costs may be unnecessary. But when dealing with average costs—as is the case when comparing different programs—the marginal revenue product can be used as a basis for distributing joint costs. When a course is given jointly for different occupations the cost would be allocated according to the relative wages of the graduates. This method implies the allocation of joint costs according to changing demands in the labor market for the output of the training.

The value of production of trainees. This can be done by timing the production process using regular workers. The same specific item is costed, using time spent by trainees. A rate of substitution of trainees' time to normal workers' time can be calculated which gives the relative wages. The relative wages can then be applied to the total time spent by the trainee minus time spent for instruction, holidays, travel, and the like. If the trainee works as part of a team only gross approximations are possible.

Outputs. To specifying the output the net benefits of the training must be determined for the individual, society, and, in the case of training in an enterprise, the firm. Net benefits are total benefits observed minus those that would accrue without the training, plus or minus changes unrelated to the person trained or the process itself.

$$B_n = B_t - B_{wt} \pm e$$
B_n = net benefits due to training
B_t = total observed benefits
B_{wt} = benefits that would have occurred without the training
e = benefits that occur because of changes outside the training system and/or the individual

Examples of B_{wt} are automatic upgrading and gains from seniority. Examples of e are economic fluctuations, windfall profits, and structural changes in industries. Net benefits are in money and intangibles. To the individual, monetary benefits include the probability of initial employment, a shorter lapse of time between completion of training and the first job, upward progress on the career ladder and in earnings (after taxes), and employment stability. Intangible benefits include job satisfaction, the gratification of having more training, a lower probability of accidents on the job, and more options in choosing an occupation if training is for broader groups of skills.

For society the benefits consist of the increased productivity of the trainee, presumably reflected by increased earnings (before taxes), and all other external benefits generally attributed to general education if it was included in the training.

Net benefits for the enterprise consist of lower turnover rates, better socialization of workers, less supervisory burdens, lower rates of rejects and accidents, and increases in productivity and production attributable to training rather than to, say, new equipment or technological change.

Choice of unit of output. The benefits and costs of a program are based on its output, but in a vocational school or training in an enterprise the output is mixed. Courses vary in content, cost, and length of training; dropouts present another difficulty. Costs per student, per student hour, per graduate, and per graduate hour are averages of outputs of a system. A comparison of the averages of two programs gives a reliable answer when the components are similarly weighted. If they are not, it may be necessary to deal with costs and outputs at a more detailed level of aggregation. *Cost-benefit and cost-effectiveness analyses.* A comparison of costs and outputs of a training system is a cost-benefit analysis when the output can be expressed as a monetary value; it is called a cost-effectiveness analysis when the major benefits are nonmonetary. In the latter case two measures are needed for each program to make a comparison. In a cost-benefit analysis the ratio of benefits to costs is a criterion for choosing one program over another, but it cannot be used as a definite criterion of cost-effectiveness because the choice of program will also depend on the marginal utility of the extra benefits compared with the marginal costs of both programs.

Each study discussed in the review of the literature was analyzed in accordance with the framework presented in this appendix. A checklist of the variables follows. The application of this analytical framework to other evaluations of vocational programs will provide a sense of the completeness and thoroughness of the studies and can be used as a yardstick for measuring the validity of applying their conclusions to other situations.

Checklist of Variables for Analyzing Evaluations of Vocational Training

A. Purpose
    1. To indicate success or failure
    2. To provide a basis for improving the program
    3. To draw comparisons
B. Coverage of study
    1. Whole systems
    2. Groups of schools or enterprises
       a. Large sample of the training system
       b. Small sample of the training system
    3. Single school or enterprise
       a. Large sample of the training system
       b. Small sample of the training system
C. Process evaluation, both quantitative and qualitative
    1. Teachers
    2. Curriculum
    3. Teaching methods
    4. Class size
    5. Equipment and materials
    6. Buildings
    7. Administration
    8. Related services (job counseling, guidance, placement)

D. Output evaluation
   1. A priori studies
      a. Cost-benefit analysis
   2. A posteriori studies
      a. Cost-benefit analysis
      b. Cost-effectiveness analysis
      c. Subjective evaluation by peers and superiors
E. Specification of inputs (trainees)
   1. Age
   2. Background
   3. Previous education
   4. Previous experience
   5. Intelligence
   6. Motivation
   7. Aptitude
   8. Sex
   9. Race
   10. Location
   11. Other
F. Selection procedures
G. Costs to individual in vocational school
   1. Fees
   2. Books and materials
   3. Travel and other incidental expenditures
   4. Opportunity cost of time in school
   5. Minus scholarships, board and room, monetary support, stipends, and other
H. Costs of training to vocational school for new or established program
   1. Salaries of teachers
   2. Salaries of administrative and maintenance personnel
   3. Buildings and equipment
   4. Materials
   5. Board and room
   6. Scholarships
   7. Incidental expenses
   8. Minus fees, other charges, and revenue from the sale of finished products
   9. Marginal and average costs
   10. Other
I. Costs of training to an enterprise for new or established program
   1. Direct costs of training program
      a. Setting up a new program

      b. Salaries of instructors
      c. Administration
      d. Consultants
      e. Buildings and equipment specifically used in training
      f. Maintenance of buildings and equipment specifically used in training
      g. Materials and books specifically used in training
      h. Other (travel, board, and meals)
      i. Marginal and average costs
  2. Indirect costs of training program
      a. Opportunity cost of time lost by personnel not directly involved in training
      b. Opportunity cost of production facilities and equipment
      c. Loss of production due to errors and spoilage
      d. Extra insurance costs
      e. Other
  3. Wages of trainees minus increased value of production attributable to trainees

J. Methods used to determine special types of cost
  1. Allocation of joint costs
  2. Evaluation of buildings and equipment
  3. Evaluation of trainees' production

K. Benefits for the individual
  1. Monetary
      a. Probability of getting the first job
      b. Time lapse between graduation and the first job
      c. Progression of after-tax earnings
      d. Employment stability
      e. Lower accident rate
  2. Intangible
      a. Job satisfaction
      b. Gratification from more education
      c. Increase of occupational options
      d. Other

L. Benefits to society
  1. Increased earnings before tax (a proxy for productivity)
  2. External benefits of general education
  3. Percentage of time employed

M. Benefits to enterprise of training programs
  1. Less supervisory burden, more disciplined work force
  2. Lower rate of turnover
  3. Better socialization of workers

    4. Increased productivity because of training (rather than new equipment)

    5. Lower rate of rejects or accidents

    6. Other

N. Choice of unit of output
1. Student
2. Graduate
3. Student hour
4. Graduate hour
5. Occupation
6. Employed graduate

O. Criterion for cost-benefit or cost-effectiveness analyses
1. Benefits > costs
2. Benefit/costs
3. Rate of return

P. General conclusions

Appendix C

A Review of the Literature

Complete references to the studies discussed in this appendix are given in the Bibliography, grouped under the same headings and listed in the same order in which they are reviewed here. The numeral in parentheses after an author's name in the text refers to the bibliographical listing of the study.

Comparative Studies of Formal Vocational Schooling and On-the-job Training

In the United States. Few studies of this type were done in the United States, and none contains data or a detailed analysis of the cost of on-the-job training. The three studies analyzed here are not parallel. One is a theoretical study based on census data. The second compares only effectiveness, and the third compares formal vocational schooling with a cooperative program that combines institutional and on-the-job training.

Mincer (1) used national census data to compare the rates of return of on-the-job training and formal schooling. He derives the cost of each kind of training from the difference in wages paid to persons with the same job but different levels of previous education. The benefits consist of lifetime earnings. The study concludes that there is no significant difference between the social rates of return of on-the-job and formal vocational school training, although the private rate of return is higher for formal schooling.

Merenda (2) compares the performance of persons trained on the job and in a formal training school in the United States Navy by using the navy's promotion test. Of the two sample groups, matched for their ability before training, the graduates of formal schools did better. The author concludes that formal schooling is a superior method of training, but this result cannot be accepted from a cost-effectiveness viewpoint since no analysis of costs was made.

Sanders (3) provides a more detailed analysis of the costs and benefits of a cooperative educational program and formal vocational schools in Springfield, Illinois. He considered most but not all of the costs and benefits to the individual and society. The study concludes that there is not much difference in the benefits of the two kinds of programs, but the fact that the costs of the formal school are much greater implies that cooperative training is more cost-effective.

This rather small number of U.S. studies comparing on-the-job training with formal vocational schooling does not lead to any definite conclusion. None of these studies can be called a careful or complete cost-benefit or cost-effectiveness analysis. Specification of trainees was far from complete; only one study considered costs to the enterprise in a systematic way; benefits such as the probability of getting the first job, satisfaction from the job, increase of occupational options, and the like were not considered. In summary, it is impossible to state from the evidence presented in the U.S. studies that training on the job is more or less cost-effective than in a formal setting.

Outside the United States. The number of studies which compare formal vocational schooling with on-the-job training elsewhere in the world is also very small. The majority come from the Soviet Union where there is a keen interest in the problem, the most specific and complete study being found in a book edited by Yagodkin (4). It compares academic vocational training with on-the-job training, using a small sample of machine operators and metal fitters from two factories. The study offers some data on the costs of on-the-job training and derives the costs of vocational schools from national averages to show that school costs are many times those of in-factory training. But the graduates of vocational schools enjoy greater benefits—faster progression in salary scales, more satisfaction on the job, lower turnover rates. Although the study does not calculate cost-benefit ratios, it concludes that formal schooling is superior to on-the-job training and recommends expansion of formal vocational schooling in the Soviet Union.

Krevnevich (5) cites a study that compares the efficiency of school-based and industry-based training for setters and fitters-repairmen for automatic production lines. The sample selected for the analysis was quite large: 4,200 workers in many factories located in six cities. Data on costs and benefits are fairly detailed. Benefits also include the value of production of students in vocational schools. Although the study does not calculate any cost-benefit ratios, it concludes that the costs of each kind of training are similar but that the benefits from training in school are greater than from on the job in terms of higher wages, more rapid promotion, and larger bonuses received for efficiency suggestions. Again it is recommended that formal vocational schooling in the Soviet Union be expanded.

In a third study Stepanov (6) compares school-based with on-the-job training of lathe operators, using a small sample in two Leningrad factories. The study does not offer data on specific costs, although it states that the costs of formal schooling are higher. Measurable benefits such as earnings and length of payback period (time needed to recoup the investment) are again found to be greater for those trained in schools, and the study concludes that training in school is more profitable than on the job.

Belkin (7) cites studies done at three mechanical engineering plants in Moscow and a few chemical plants in Lisichansk to compare vocational school graduates with those trained in the plants. He does not mention costs but points out the benefits in terms of increased productivity and earnings and the speed of advancement on the job. The studies favor vocational school graduates and Belkin's conclusion is again to expand formal vocational schools.

In another article Belkin (8) discusses training workers in vocational schools as against on the job in the Soviet Union as a whole. The evaluation is qualitative and concludes that vocational training programs in schools have to be expanded to provide the skilled workers necessary to operate the increasingly complex and automated machinery of industry. The major justification for expanding formal vocational schools is that they provide the theoretical understanding required for technologically advanced production.

A comparative study conducted by CIRF (9) of methods of training skilled metalworkers in Europe does not deal with the cost-effectiveness of different training methods but provides a qualitative assessment of training in Belgium (primarily in schools), West Germany (a combination of school and apprenticeship), the United Kingdom (a loosely organized apprenticeship system), and the Netherlands (school and in-plant training). The conclusions are that there is a common trend toward increased vocational training in the plants, that it is wasteful when workers specialize too narrowly, and that wage classifications and formal training requirements hamper mobility of workers climbing the job ladder. The study also points out the difficulties of making international comparisons of vocational education—even the definition of skilled worker in the metal trade was a sticky point in the comparison.

A few studies try to calculate the cost-benefit ratios or the income attributed to different types of education and training in general. Kullmer (10) used a one percent sample of a national census in West Germany to calculate the relationships between nine types of training and the net income by age and sex. The types of education ranked by income from high to low are: university, technical college, teacher training college (except in the 14–29 age group where this type ranks lower), business training, technical school, full-time vocational school, practical training only, in-plant training, and no training. The study does not compare incomes with costs.

In connection with an evaluation of the cost of in-plant training in West Germany, Winterhager (11) states that training in schools is cheaper than in the factory because the factory has lower student-teacher ratios.

Blaug (12) conducted a pilot study in England to compare the costs and benefits of six levels of education and three types of programs. The pilot study provided the data to calculate the earnings of employees by age at five electrical engineering firms, but cost figures were derived from general national studies. The study provides no definite conclusions except that more detailed data are needed.

What can be learned from this group of studies? No country so far seems to have produced adequate answers to the question of the relative efficiency of formal vocational schooling and on-the-job training for its own system, let alone provided conclusions that can be translated or exported abroad. The studies done in the Soviet Union tend to consider vocational school training more cost-effective than that on the job, although no cost-benefit or cost-effectiveness ratios are given, and their calculations of costs should be viewed with skepticism. All these studies merely imply that in general factory workers with formal vocational training may be more efficient than those trained on the job, but there is no explicit relationship between increased efficiency and costs. Even in the area of costs there is disagreement. The general consensus is that on-the-job training is cheaper than in vocational schools, but Winterhager mentions that training in schools is cheaper than in the factory because of a lower student-teacher ratio.

Comparative Studies of Vocational and General Secondary Schools

In the United States. The relative cost-effectiveness of academic and vocational high schools has sparked some debate in the United States. A search of the literature yielded five major studies comparing general secondary with vocational schools.

Hu (13) uses questionnaire data to compare regular and vocational high school graduates in three cities. Results are corrected by a two-thirds non-response bias. Costs and benefit analyses are fairly complete. Benefits include assessment of noneconomic factors such as voting behavior and economic aspirations. The study does not conclude that vocational education is more cost-effective but advocates that more funds be allocated for vocational rather than nonvocational curricula in high schools.

Schriver (14) compares vocational school with high school graduates in Tennessee using two rigorously matched groups drawn from a 25 percent random sample. Costs per hour of instruction and per student in each type of school were calculated. Benefits include such factors as employment stability and mobility. The study concludes that vocational education has advantages over academic high school and that the rate of return of vocational schooling is highest for students with the lowest aptitudes.

Corrazzini (15) compares vocational and academic high schools in Worcester, Massachusetts, by sampling 12 neighboring firms that employ their graduates. Most of the important cost elements of each kind of schooling are considered; benefits include earnings, a lower dropout rate, and geographic mobility. The study concludes that vocational education is at best only marginally profitable and that its extra cost may not be justified by these small benefits.

Taussig's study (16) compares vocational and academic high schools in New York City. Most important costs are considered except joint costs, which the author says are too difficult to estimate. Benefits are inferred from a postcard survey of graduates with no follow-up or correction for nonresponse bias. No calculation of cost-benefit was done. The study concludes that investment in vocational schools has not rendered significantly greater benefits than regular secondary schools and therefore should not be recommended for the future.

A study by Paulter (17) compares vocational secondary school graduates, vocational school dropouts, and nonvocational high school graduates not continuing their education. The comparison is based only on benefits and not on costs. The criteria for benefits were the time necessary to get the first job, earnings, and employment stability. The study did not find major differences among the three groups.

These studies offer fairly complete analyses of costs and benefits, yet the conclusions are contradictory: two studies conclude that vocational schooling is more profitable than general secondary schooling, while two reach the opposite conclusion, and one concludes that there is no difference.

Outside the United States. Al-Bukhari (18) evaluates public secondary industrial (vocational) schools in Jordan. Ninety graduates from two institutions, plus employers, teachers, and nongraduates were interviewed. The study finds that the curricula do not correspond to industry's needs because only 28 percent of the graduates were using skills they had learned at the schools. Cost-benefit ratios for vocational school graduates are 1.6:1, and 6.7:1 for general academic school graduates. Al-Bukhari recommends that the two kinds of schools be combined to give both kinds of education to all students.

Lourdesamy (19) in a follow-up study of graduates of vocational schools in Malaysia found that their average starting salaries were lower than those of graduates from the general secondary school and that unemployment rates were higher. This together with the fact that vocational school costs were 8.5 percent higher than those of secondary schools clearly implies that vocational schools compare unfavorably with the general academic.

These two studies seem to reflect the prevalent attitude in developing countries that formal vocational schooling has a higher cost-benefit ratio than does general schooling. The results do not address the basic question of cost-effectiveness, however. A major complaint against the vocational school is that the curriculum is not adapted to the demands of the economy; hence graduates do not find ready employment. But this is an external inefficiency—a combination of factors has been chosen for a program whose output is not highly valued in the market. The studies do not consider the problem of internal efficiency, which is the other side of the coin—given the objective of producing a particular output, how to choose a combination of factors that will minimize the costs of a program.

Evaluations of Formal Vocational Schools

These studies do not compare different types of schooling but generally make a qualitative evaluation of vocational school training with the aim of improving it.

In the United States. Somers (20) compares three educational levels (high school, post-high school, and junior college) and six programs (vocational and academic) using cost-benefit analysis. Cost figures were taken from sundry studies, while benefits were determined from a questionnaire sent to a national stratified random sample, which suffered from a low response rate (25 to 56 percent). Monetary and nonmonetary benefits were appraised, including the socioeconomic status of the respondent's job. The study concludes that the job-relatedness of a person's schooling and the socioeconomic status, not the wages, are the major determinants of the level of satisfaction with a job.

Another U.S. study focused on Connecticut vocational-technical schools (21) to provide a basis for recommending improvements in the public vocational school system. The sample was adequate. The study found that a large proportion of graduates were working at jobs unrelated to their training and recommended better liaison between industry and the schools. Recommendations also included the improvement of courses, counseling, and placement services.

Outside the United States. Binninger (22) evaluates the French system of vocational education and concludes that it fails to teach enough general skills and knowledge. No sample of respondents is specified. The main criticism of vocational schools is that workers trained in them are unable to learn quickly the new production methods demanded by technological changes. The study concludes that the solution is to update the curriculum and use modern equipment and teaching methods.

Belkin (23), in a short article, points out that the 25-year trend in the Soviet Union has been toward a growing proportion of vocational school graduates in the labor force. According to his findings workers with these extra years of formal education adapt better to technological change and have lower rates of rejects in production.

Sokolov (24) describes and evaluates several methods of combining the training given in vocational schools with general secondary education. The study shows that graduates of a three-year school with a combined program were promoted more quickly than graduates of the regular two-year vocational school. The drawback is that the cost of the three-year program is of course higher.

Grüner (25) evaluates the public industrial schools (Berufsfachschulen, BFS) in West Germany. Ninety-six firms responded to a questionnaire. Their general opinion of the BFS was favorable, but the firms noted a lack of relevant practical experience among graduates. The author concludes that the post-BFS apprenticeship periods could be shortened if the schools could provide more practical experience.

Any attempt to draw conclusions from the foregoing evaluations of vocational schooling is deterred by the diversity of systems and experiments. Nevertheless the authors of these studies share the conviction that formal vocational schooling is an important and valuable part of their countries' educational systems. They also seem to have touched on a common need to satisfy industry's dual requirements for workers who not only are able to learn new production methods but also have had practical experience with current methods. General and theoretical education is necessary for the former, and actual practical work is necessary for the latter; the question is how best to allocate the limited amount of training time and teaching resources. Unfortunately the studies in this survey do not seem to have confronted this question directly enough to serve as examples for planners in countries at different stages of development.

Evaluations of Nonschool Vocational Programs

These studies evaluate specific training programs given outside the formal school system. Naturally most of them include some on-the-job training. The programs range from adult training using school facilities after hours to on-the-job training run primarily by firms.

In the United States. The largest system of adult vocational training programs in the United States was established under the Manpower Development and Training Act (MDTA). Several studies deal with its effectiveness both in general and in regard to specific training courses.

Borus (26) evaluates the MDTA program in Connecticut. Most of the important costs and benefits are carefully considered; cost-benefit ratios for the economy, the government, and the individual are all greater than one, with that for the economy the highest, followed by that for government. Borus also found unemployment to be decreased by training only when there are vacancies in the labor market.

A study by Main (27) focuses on the income and employment of graduates of the nationwide system of institutional job-training centers established by the MDTA. The sample consisted of 1,200 former trainees. There is no analysis of costs. Results show no significant difference in wages between those who completed the program and those who did not. The employment period for those who completed the program was longer by an estimated 13 to 23 percent, whereas for dropouts it increased by only 7 to 19 percent.

Mangum (28) also evaluates the whole system of the MDTA. He measures its total costs and benefits to society in terms of increased productivity and lower unemployment rates. Based on the net additional earnings of all enrollees during the first year after training, the MDTA cost-benefit ratio for the federal government is 3.28 for on-the-job training and 1.78 for institutional training.

There are also a series of cost-benefit and cost-effectiveness studies of other training programs in the United States. Cain (29) offers cost-benefit estimates for the Job Corps from a postcard survey of a group of white Southern males. Most of the important costs are considered, and benefits consist of increased earnings and various nonmonetary benefits. The author also provides a cost-benefit ratio for different levels of educational achievement. He concludes that the Job Corps does increase lifetime earnings by teaching reading and math as well as through vocational training. With fewer dropouts and a fuller use of the facilities, Cain predicts that the cost-benefit ratio would greatly increase.

Bateman (30) evaluates the Work Experience and Training Program, a cooperative system which includes some on-the-job training. He analyzes many of the important costs and benefits for the government and society. As did Main in his study of the MDTA, Bateman finds no significant increase in monthly earnings as a result of the program, but many previously unemployed participants were able to get jobs.

Kirby (31) examines an experimental vocational education program called the Training and Technology Project. Many of the important costs and benefits are considered, and the rate of return on the government's investment is found to be 20 percent. In addition society achieved a more efficient allocation of labor because the skills taught were actually needed by industries in the area.

Kraft (32), in evaluating the cost-effectiveness of two vocational-technical training programs at centers in Florida, considers most of the important costs and benefits (including nonmonetary benefits) and determines ratios and rates of return. Since these measures were positive, the author considers the programs successful.

Scott (33) determines the economic effectiveness of an on-the-job training program for Indians in Oklahoma on the basis of a sample of 78 respondents who were trained in nine firms. Some of the important costs and monetary benefits were considered. High private and social cost-benefit ratios were found, and the program was judged effective. The study recommends shortening the training periods, most of which appeared to be longer than necessary to develop the skills required.

Roberts (34) evaluates a preapprenticeship program in Washington, D.C., that was designed to bring more blacks into the building trades. The average cost to the government is compared with benefits from increased earnings and employment stability. Half of the 143 participants completing the program were in an apprenticeship program a year later, and their wages had increased 55 percent as against 25 percent for those of the control group of nonselected applicants. Because these results compare favorably with those of other training programs the author considers the experiment a success. The study also includes a series of evaluations of nonschool vocational programs that refer to costs and benefits in a qualitative manner.

Doyle (35) gathered comments from an unspecified sample of union- and corporation-sponsored apprenticeship programs to make a qualitative evaluation. He finds that instructors and apprentices begrudge the time they must spend together because only monetary incentives are offered. The length of time involved in learning a skill is determined not by the aptitude or performance of the apprentice but by a fixed rule. An improvement in nonmonetary incentives would also lower the costs of training to a firm. Doyle recommends improving and expanding apprenticeship programs.

Grell (36) focuses on a group of MDTA programs given in public schools in Lincoln, Nebraska, and bases his study on a questionnaire sent to 389 students of the clerical, practical nursing, and dental assistant programs, and to 123 employers. No costs or quantitative benefits are considered. He reports general satisfaction with the programs.

Perlman (37) bases his evaluation of on-the-job training programs on interviews with 245 firms in Milwaukee, Wisconsin, 150 of which offer formal training. He describes the curricula and methods of these programs and the selection procedure for trainees. There is no specific analysis of costs and benefits. He finds that many vocational school graduates have to be retrained on the production line and therefore recommends that vocational schools concentrate on general skills, including language and math. He also observes that very few firms have formal ongoing training programs; most are set up for current needs and keep the worker active in production.

Tuttle (38) presents a qualitative evaluation of a cooperative training program in Des Moines, Iowa, based on interviews with 135 graduates and 30 of their employers. The graduates were generally satisfied with the curriculum of their training, and 62 percent were in jobs related to their training. Employers were also satisfied. The program was therefore considered a success.

Although nearly all these studies show that the programs were successful on a cost-effectiveness or qualitative basis, most do not present a comprehensive analysis of costs. This is especially true for programs that have a large component of on-the-job training. There are also no comparisons of cost and benefit or cost-effectiveness of different modes of training to enable decisionmakers to choose among training alternatives.

Outside the United States. With few exceptions evaluations of adult training programs in developing countries also lack comprehensive analyses. The first group of studies is made up of evaluations of national training systems. The study by Horowitz and Zymelman (39) looks at the Rapid Retraining System of Adult Vocational Education in Brazil. A sample of 5,000 out of 57,000 enrollees was interviewed. Graduates, teachers, and administrators gave a complete evaluation of the training process. Almost all the important costs of the program to the government and benefits to the individual (including nonmonetary) were considered. The authors conclude that this mode of training is effective because most of the graduates were employed and well regarded by their superiors. Costs per graduate were also low because the program took advantage of existing excess capacity of buildings and equipment of industries and schools.

A similar six-month accelerated course of adult vocational training in Portugal is studied by de Carvalho (40), who used a sample of 415 trainees in two series of courses at one training center in Lisbon. The costs of the two series were compared with the estimated increases in productivity, and the rate of return was found to be 25 to 30 percent, the payback period 328 working days. The author concludes that this program is quite successful.

Chakravarti (41) evaluates the social return from a program in India to train unskilled workers in the heavy electrical industry, a public-sector enterprise. He uses a sample of 1,770 workers enrolled in a two-year program. Many of the important costs to the firm and the monetary benefits to society (increased productivity) are considered. Rates of return are calculated using assumptions about shadow wages and training costs, including the domestic and world-market prices. The rates vary between 3 and 48 percent, but the author concludes that since most are higher than 6 percent the program is profitable.

An a priori study by Arrigazzi (42) was made to determine whether or not to expand some vocational training programs offered by INACAP, the National Training Institute of Chile. Some of the important costs and most of the important monetary benefits are considered. The report predicts a rate of return on investment in the expansion of vocational education from 30 to 50 percent.

Many studies evaluate off-the-job training in European countries. Ziderman (43) discusses the governmental vocational training centers for adults in the United Kingdom, analyzing data collected by the government. Most of the important costs and benefits (monetary and nonmonetary) are considered. He develops criteria for the rate of return and payback period, from which he concludes that the programs at the centers have net positive benefits to society. He urges that a more detailed survey follow his, using control groups, a specified sample, and analysis of indirect effects.

"La Formation professionnelle des adultes" (44) is an evaluation of the French system of vocational training for adults. No sample is specified. The study describes the system and concludes that it is a success because many graduates found employment and two-thirds of them are now working in jobs for which they were trained. The expansion of the system is recommended.

The study by Fenger (45) is a qualitative examination of the system of plant schools in West Germany designed to provide a secondary vocational education, including general courses and theory, to young people continuing their compulsory education. Data come from 23 large firms that operate such schools and 100 other firms with apprenticeship programs but no theoretical training. Fenger concludes that the plant schools are successful from the students' point of view but rather expensive for the firms. The 100 firms expressed general satisfaction with the training given by the much larger system of public vocational schools, and Fenger therefore expects that there will not be much pressure to expand the plant-school system.

Reinermann (46) summarizes the qualitative criticisms and defenses of the apprenticeship program in West Germany. No sample is specified. The author concludes that there is still an important place in Common Market countries for apprenticeship programs in certain skills such as plumbing, electrical installation, and automobile mechanics.

Two excellent European studies of specific training programs are Thomas (47) and Winterhager (11). Thomas examines the benefits of an improved training program in a clothing factory in the United Kingdom. He compares the presumably haphazard and unscientific training method before improvements with the new system established by a group of consultants who studied the factory's production line, prepared a manual of instruction, and trained experienced workers in teaching methods. Costs and benefits are analyzed in detail. The high cost-benefit ratio carefully calculated by the author leads clearly to the conclusion that other factories should borrow the same ideas for their training programs. Thomas points out that 75 percent of the benefit to the firm in increased production results from the lower rate of turnover among graduates from the new program, which indicates greater satisfaction with their jobs.

Winterhager's evaluation of the cost of comprehensive in-plant training programs in West Germany has already been mentioned. All the important costs of these programs (using a sample of three firms) are considered; benefits are not, although different turnover rates associated with the training are given. The author finds that the cost per student is higher in the plant programs than in a vocational school because of lower student-teacher ratios, the high cost of teaching equipment, and student financial aid. No clear relationship is seen between the cost of training and the turnover rate of trainees.

Castro (48) compares costs per student hour of special training programs and formal vocational schools in Brazil. Data were collected from a sample of establishments and schools, but no definite conclusions were reached. In some cases the cost of training in schools exceeded that in establishments, while the reverse was true in other cases.

A review of the mixed studies in this group underscores the variety of training systems, each with its own advantages and drawbacks. No definite conclusion can be drawn about any of the results. Only specific studies such as those of Thomas and Winterhager provide a detailed analysis. In general the broader the system under analysis the less specific the conclusions that are drawn.

Miscellaneous Studies of Factors Influencing the Effectiveness of Vocational Training

The last category of this survey includes several studies whose subject falls under one of the previous categories but whose main goal is to analyze the circumstances that affect the rate of return of different kinds of training programs. They point to such things as the state of the labor market, personal characteristics of the trainee, and the effect of the first job on a graduate's earning expectations.

Hardin (49) analyzes several manpower development (MDTA) programs in Michigan. He compares cost-benefit ratios for different courses and different characteristics of trainees and the labor market. Costs were quite carefully determined for individuals and state and federal governments. The increase in disposable income is used to measure benefits to the individual, and pretax income to determine benefits to society. Multivariate analysis isolates the increases from other causes such as a favorable labor market or personal characteristics. Hardin finds that short courses give the best returns and recommends that they be expanded to include more demographic and occupational groups than at present.

Rawlins (50) compares four manpower programs for disadvantaged youth: the Job Corps, MDTA institutional centers, the Neighborhood Youth Corps (NYC) program for school dropouts, and MDTA on-the-job training. He examines one program of each kind in the Los Angeles area. Some of the important costs are considered; the benefits are increased earnings. Rawlins finds that the kind of program seems to have no effect on earnings, but that earnings increase the longer a trainee attends the program. The Job Corps' strong point is its good counseling effort; the NYC's special benefit is that it encourage youths to get academic credentials which may be important in the future. On-the-job training programs are good when the labor market is such that there are openings for trainees.

Gubins (51) compares the cost-benefit ratios of an MDTA program in the black ghetto of Baltimore, Maryland, with those of larger populations, including an analysis of the effects of age and educational attainment. His sample of 108 graduates represents a 33.8 percent response rate; the control group comprises all applicants to the program. Most of the important costs to the government and individuals are considered, while benefits consist of earnings. Gubins finds that there are substantial payoffs to the economy and society from training hard-core unemployed ghetto residents. The cost-benefit ratio is greater for persons younger than 22 than for those older, and greater for those with less than nine years of education than for those with more, although the training is beneficial to trainees regardless of age, sex, amount of education, or the discount rate used in the calculation. He adds that the amount of investment in this MDTA program could be expanded two or three times, and the cost-benefit ratio would still be significantly high.

Schriver (52) uses samples from other studies to analyze the effects of the personal characteristics of the trainee on the rate of return to vocational training. The study concludes that the rate of return is higher for persons who had a low IQ, were married, had additional training, but only 15 months or less at the area vocational school.

In a pilot study for a larger project Greenberg (53) analyzes the effect of an enrollee's first job on his future performance. He sampled 289 graduates of four different Los Angeles training programs who were hired by 16 firms, but he is not confident of the representativeness of the sample. No costs were analyzed, but monetary benefits were compared for carefully specified characteristics. Greenberg finds that the type of firm is the strongest variable in determining the wage rates of the first job. Being married, older, and non-Negro all have positive associations with wages, while being female or having a Spanish surname have negative associations. On-the-job training programs are significantly better than other kinds with respect to starting salaries.

Löwe (54) compares good and poor vocational school pupils at several schools in West Germany and finds that the poor pupils suffer primarily from a lack of motivation. They are not as sure of their aptitudes and interests as the good pupils, who were encouraged by a stable family life and urged by parents and teachers to explore many different fields.

What is clear from the work of this group of authors is that a training program cannot be evaluated by a cost-benefit analysis alone and then applied without reservation to all parts of the population or all geographic areas. Proper planning will always require careful consideration of the personal characteristics of the trainees and the conditions of the labor market in the area. None of the studies listed here take account of these factors in a systematic way.

Bibliography

Evaluation Studies of Vocational Education

Comparative Studies of Formal Vocational Schooling and On-the-job Training

1. Mincer, Jacob. "On-the-Job Training: Costs, Returns, and Some Implications," *Journal of Political Economy,* Vol. 70, No. 5, Pt. 2 (October 1962), Supplement, pp. 50–79.

2. Merenda, Peter. "The Relative Effectiveness of Formal School and On-the-Job Methods of Training Apprentices in Naval Occupations," *Personnel Psychology,* Vol. 11, No. 3, 1958, pp. 379–82.

3. Sanders, Lester Earl. *A Comparison of Two Methods of Preparing Youth for Employment: Cooperative Occupational Education versus the Preparatory Vocational-Technical School.* Columbia, Mo.: University of Missouri, 1967.

4. Yagodkin, V.N., ed. *Economic Problems of the Training of Skilled Workers under Contemporary Conditions.* Moscow: Izdatel'stvo Moskovskovo Universiteta, 1967, Chap. 10.

5. Krevnevich, V. "Vesproizvodstvo rabochikh kadrov" [On Training the Labor Force], *Ekonomicheskaya Gazeta,* Moscow, Vol. 35, No. 42 (October 1967), pp. 17–18.

6. Stepanov, S., J. Gribovskiy, and G. Ivanov. "Ob ekonomicheskoi effektivnosti podgotovki rabochikh-metallistov" [Economic Effectiveness of the Training of Metal Workers], Professional'no-tekhnicheskoe Obrazovanie, Moscow, Vol. 23, No. 3 (March 1966), pp. 30–31.

7. Belkin, V.B. "25 let sistemy professional'no-technicheskovo obrazovaniya" [25 Years of Vocational-Technical Education], *Ekonomicheskaya Gazeta,* Moscow, Vol. 33, No. 39 (29 September 1965), pp. 10–11.

8. Belkin, V.B. *The Division of Labor and Training of Skilled Workers in the U.S.S.R.* Moscow: Izdatel'stvo Vyshaya Shkola, 1966.

9. CIRF, International Labour Office. *Training for Progress,* Geneva, Vol. 4, No. 2, 1965.

10. Kullmer, H., and W. Krug. "Beziehungen zwischen beruflicher Ausbildung und Nettoeinkommen der ausgebildeten Personen" [The Relationship between Vocational Training and Net Income], *Wirtschaft und Statistik,* Wiesbaden, No. 10 (October 1967), pp. 570–76.

11. Winterhager, W.D. *Kosten und Finanzierung der beruflichen Bildung— eine wirtschaftstheoretische Analyse mit empirischen Daten zur Lehrlingsausbildung in der Industrie* [Theoretical and Empirical Analysis of the Cost of Vocational Training, with Particular Reference to the Financial and Input-Output Aspects of Apprenticeships in Plant Training]. Stuttgart: Ernst Klett Verlag, 1969.

12. Blaug, Mark, Maurice Peston, and Adrian Ziderman. *The Utilization of Educated Manpower in Industry: A Preliminary Report.* London: Oliver and Boyd, 1967.

Comparative Studies of Vocational and General Secondary Schools

13. Hu, Teh-Wei, Maw Lin Lee, Ernst Stromsdorfer, and J.J. Kaufman. *A Cost-Effectiveness Study of Vocational Education.* University Park: Institute for Research on Human Resources, Pennsylvania State University, March 1969.

14. Schriver, William R., and Roger I. Bowlby. *The Effects of Vocational Training on Labor Force Experience: An Analysis of the Tennessee Area Vocational Technical School System.* Memphis: State University, Tennessee Center for Manpower Studies, February 1971.

15. Corrazzini, Arthur J. "The Decision to Invest in Vocational Education: An Analysis of Costs and Benefits," *Journal of Human Resources,* Vol. 3, Supplement, 1968, pp. 38–120.

16. Taussig, Michael K. "An Economic Analysis of Vocational Education in the New York City High Schools," *Journal of Human Resources,* Vol. 3, Supplement, 1968, pp. 59–87.

17. Paulter, Albert J. "A Follow-up Study of Vocational High School Graduates in Erie County, New York, with Implications for Vocational

Education." Ph.D. dissertation, State University of New York at Buffalo, 1967.

18. Al-Bukhari, N.M.A. "Issues in Occupational Education and Training: A Case Study in Jordan." Stanford, Calif.: Stanford International Development Education Center, Stanford University, 1968 (mimeo).

19. Lourdesamy, I. "Vocational Education in Malaysia: A Case Study in Development Administrations." Ph.D. dissertation, University of Pittsburgh, 1972.

Evaluations of Formal Vocational Schools

20. Somers, G.G., L.M. Sharp, T. Myint, and S.F. Meives. *The Effectiveness of Vocational and Technical Programs: A National Follow-up Survey.* Madison, Wis.: University of Wisconsin, Center for Studies in Vocational and Technical Education, 1971.

21. University Research Institute of Connecticut, Inc. *Five and Ten Year Follow-up Study of Connecticut State Vocational-Technical Schools, Graduates of Classes of 1958 and 1963, Final Report.* Hartford, Conn.: State Department of Education, March 1969.

22. Binninger, M. "The Opinion of a PTA on the CET in World of Changing Techniques," *Syndicalisme universitaire,* Paris, No. 356 (10 February 1965), pp. 1362–66, and No. 357 (17 February 1965), pp. 1371–77.

23. Belkin, V.B. "Ekonomicheskie problemy podgotovki rabochikh kadrov" [The Economic Problems of Training Skilled Workers], *Planovoe Khozyaistvo,* Moscow, Vol. 45, No. 5 (May 1968), pp. 25–34.

24. Sokolov, A.G. "Vozmozhnosti Soyedineniya Obshchevo i Professional'no-tekhnicheskovo Obrazovaniya" [The Possibility of Combining General Education with Vocational Training], *Sovyetskaya Pedagogika,* Moscow, Vol. 23, No. 3 (March 1969), pp. 39–46.

25. Grüner, G. *Die gewerblich-technischen Berufsfachschulen in der Bundesrepublik Deutschland* [Full-time Industrial Vocational Schools in the Federal Republic of Germany]. Studien zur Arbeits- und Berufspädagogik, Deutsches Institut für Internationale Pädagogische Forschung. Berlin: Verlag Julius Beltz, 1968, Vol. 4

Evaluations of Nonschool Vocational Programs

26. Borus, Michael E. "A Benefit-Cost Analysis of the Economic Effectiveness of Retraining the Unemployed," *Yale Economic Essays,* Vol. 4, No. 2 (Fall 1964), pp. 371–427.

27. Main, Earl D. "A Nationwide Evaluation of MDTA Institutional Job

Training," *Journal of Human Resources,* Vol. 3, No. 2 (Spring 1968), pp. 159–70.

28. Mangum, Garth L. *Contributions and Costs of Manpower Development and Training.* Policy Papers in Human Resources and Industrial Relations, No. 5. Ann Arbor, Mich.: Institute of Labor and Industrial Relations, University of Michigan–Wayne State University, and the National Manpower Policy Task Force, 1967.

29. Cain, Glen G. "Benefit/Cost Estimates for Job Corps." Discussion Paper Series, No. 9. Madison, Wis.: Institute for Research on Poverty, The University of Wisconsin, 1967 (mimeo).

30. Bateman, Worth. "An Application of Cost-Benefit Analysis to the Work-Experience and Training Program," *American Economic Review, Papers and Proceedings,* Vol. 57, No. 2 (May 1967), pp. 80–90.

31. Kirby, Frederick C., and Paul A. Castagna. *Benefit-Cost Analysis of TAT* (Training and Technology Project), Phase I, Special Report. Oak Ridge, Tenn.: Atomic Energy Commission, July 1969.

32. Kraft, Richard H.P. *Cost-Effectiveness Analysis of Vocational-Technical Education Programs: A Pilot Study, Final Report (October 14, 1968, to June 30, 1969).* Tallahassee, Fla.: Florida State University, Educational Systems and Planning Center, June 1969.

33. Scott, L.C. "The Economic Effectiveness of On-The-Job Training. The Experience of the Bureau of Indian Affairs in Oklahoma (1960–1966)," *Industrial and Labor Relations Review,* Vol. 23, No. 2 (January 1970), pp. 220–36.

34. Roberts, Markley. "Labor Sponsored Preapprenticeship Training: What Is the Payoff?" *Labor Law Journal,* Vol. 21, No. 10 (October 1970), pp. 663–67.

35. Doyle, Lawrence F. "An Evaluation of Apprenticeship: Growth or Stagnation," *Training and Development Journal,* Vol. 21, No. 10 (October 1967), pp. 2–12.

36. Grell, Darrell Dean. *An Evaluation of the Manpower Development and Training Program in the Lincoln, Nebraska, Public Schools.* Lincoln: University of Nebraska Teachers' College, 1967.

37. Perlman, Richard. *On-the-Job Training in Milwaukee—Nature, Extent and Relationship to Vocational Education.* Madison, Wis.: Industrial Relations Research Institute, Wisconsin University, June 1969.

38. Tuttle, David Chester. *A Follow-up Study of Graduates' and Employers' Opinions of a Cooperating Training Program.* Research Study No. 1. Denver: Colorado State College, 1965.

39. Horowitz, M., and Manuel Zymelman. *The Brazilian Intensive Training Program: Report and Methodology.* Montevideo: CINTERFOR, 1967.

40. de Carvalho, Esteves Odete. "Comparative Analysis of the Social and Economic Impact of the Vocational Training Given in the First 14 FPA Courses and in the 20 Subsequent Courses," *Boletim Bimestral do Fundo de Desenvolvimento da Mão-de-Obra*, Lisbon, Supplement, No. 23 (January 1969), pp. 41–48.

41. Chakravarti, A. "Social Profitability of Training Unskilled Workers in the Public Sector in India," *Oxford Economic Papers*, London, Vol. 24, No. 1 (March 1972), pp. 111–23.

42. Arrigazzi, Lucila. "Evaluating the Expansion of a Vocational Training Programme," *Educational Cost-Analysis in Action*. UNESCO, International Institute of Educational Planning, July 1972.

43. Ziderman, A. "Costs and Benefits of Adult Retraining in the United Kingdom," *Economica*, London, Vol. 36, No. 144 (November 1969), pp. 363–76.

44. "La Formation professionnelle des adultes: Loi No. 71-575 du 16 Juillet 1971 portant organisation de la formation professionnelle," *Journal officiel de la République française*, Paris, Vol. 103, No. 164 (17 July 1971), pp. 7035–41.

45. Fenger, H. *Betriebsberufsschulen in der Bundesrepublik Deutschland* [Plant Vocational Schools in the Federal Republic of Germany]. Freiburg im Breisgau: Jahrbuch für Wirtschafts- und Sozialpädagogik. 1969.

46. Reinermann, W. "Die Handwerkslehre im Kreuzfeuer der Sozialkritik." [Artisan Training under the Cross Fire of Social Criticism]. *Berufserziehung zwischen Tradition und Fortschritt*. Cologne: Wolfgang Stratenwerth, 1967, pp. 92–121.

47. Thomas, Brinley, John Moxham, and J.A.G. Jones. "A Cost-Benefit Analysis of Industrial Training," *British Journal of Industrial Relations*, Vol. 7, No. 2 (July 1969), pp. 231–64.

48. Castro, Claudio, Pereira de Assio, and Oliveira Sandra Furtado. *Ensino Técnico: Desempenho e Custos*. Rio de Janeiro: IPEA/INPES, 1972.

Miscellaneous Studies of Factors Influencing the Effectiveness of Vocational Training

49. Hardin, Einar, and Michael E. Borus. *Economic Benefits and Costs of Retraining Courses in Michigan*. East Lansing: Michigan State University, 1969.

50. Rawlins, V.L. "Manpower Programs for Disadvantaged Youths," *Industrial Relations*, Berkeley, Vol. 11, No. 2 (May 1972), pp. 184–97.

51. Gubins, Samuel. "The Impact of Age and Education on the Effectiveness of Training: A Benefit-Cost Analysis." Ph.D. dissertation, Johns Hopkins University, Baltimore, Md., 1970.

52. Schriver, William R., and Roger I. Bowlby. *An Analysis of Differential Benefits from Vocational Training, Final Report.* Memphis, Tenn.: State University, April 1971.

53. Greenberg, D.H. "Employing the Training-Program Enrollee: An Analysis of Employer Personnel Records," *Industrial and Labor Relations Review,* Ithaca, N.Y., Vol. 24, No. 4 (July 1971), pp. 554–71.

54. Löwe, Hans. "Über Ursachen und Bedingungen des unterschiedlichen Leistungsverhaltens bei Berufsschülern" [Causes of and Conditions Influencing Different Attitudes toward Work among Vocational School Pupils], *Berufsbildung,* Berlin, Vol. 18, No. 10 (October 1964), pp. 448–92; No. 11 (November 1964), pp. 536–38; No. 12 (December 1964), pp. 586–89.